**Praise for *The Three-Box Solution Playbook***

"*The Three-Box Solution Playbook* is a practical and cogent guide on innovation and execution. It's a must-read for every manager seeking organizational renewal and working to drive meaningful and sustained impact."

> —**ANTHONY LLANO**, Regional Manager, Distribution Centers, Western USA/Hispano America, Deere & Company

"Vijay Govindarajan has done it again. *The Three-Box Solution Playbook* will inspire large companies all over the globe to truly innovate. Govindarajan's framework is terrific."

> —**LINDA YATES**, founder and CEO, Mach49

"*The Three-Box Solution Playbook* is an excellent guide to how organizations can grow, disrupt, pivot, and survive in times of deep uncertainty and change. Pragmatic and practical, Govindarajan and Tangri's playbook makes the seemingly insurmountable challenge of getting a breakthrough idea off the ground seem surmountable."

> —**RAGNHILD ØYE**, Change Partner, Talent, Leadership, and Capability, FTSE 100 Leading Industrial Technology Company

**Praise for *The Three-Box Solution***

"Govindarajan's book is both challenging and easy to understand, offering numerous examples—from IBM to GE to Hasbro—of companies that have made this concept work."

> —*Success* Magazine

"*The Three-Box Solution* is clearly presented, with illuminating case studies from a variety of organizations helping to explain the ideas."

> —*The Globe and Mail*

"When we read *The Three-Box Solution* and Govindarajan describes the experiences from leaders of Hasbro, Tata, IBM, United Rentals, and Mahindra & Mahindra, among others, we get inspired to find our own balance between these three innovation areas: preservation, destruction, and creation. *The Three-Box Solution* helps leaders come into harmony with an ageless rhythm that creates sustainable prosperity."

—*InnovationManagement* (innovationmanagement.se)

"With case studies from toy manufacturer Hasbro, coffee maker Keurig, Tata Consultancy Services, and even a church reinventing itself, *The Three-Box Solution* makes a good, breezy read."

—*The Times of India*

"*The Three-Box Solution* kick-started our journey into innovation, powerfully shifting our mind-set, and it continues to guide and propel our new product development."

—**T. J. ELLIOTT**, former Vice President and Chief Learning Officer, Educational Testing Service

"Transformation of any significance is inherently complicated, and that is why the simplicity and practicality of *The Three-Box Solution* has proven such an elegant framework for Hasbro's journey from a toy and game manufacturer to a global toy and entertainment company."

—**DOLPH JOHNSON**, Executive Vice President and Chief Global Human Resources Officer, Hasbro

"Simple, powerful, and purposeful."

—**JEFFREY R. IMMELT**, former Chairman and CEO, General Electric

"*The Three-Box Solution* presents a simple yet powerful framework to simultaneously optimize continuous process improvement and breakthrough innovation. Inspiring for management executives."

—**ZHANG RUIMIN**, founder, Chairman, and CEO, Haier Group

"Govindarajan's *The Three-Box Solution* provides a framework for balancing the imperatives of the present with the demands of the future. It is a construct that permeates all our strategic thinking."

—**ANAND G. MAHINDRA**, Chairman and Managing Director, Mahindra Group

"If your company needs to stop doing what it's done and branch out in new and profitable ways, this is the book for you."

—**MARSHALL GOLDSMITH**, *New York Times* and *Wall Street Journal*–bestselling author, *Triggers*

"*The Three-Box Solution* is a superb guidance manual for anyone formulating and driving a long-term company strategy. An excellent resource for managers and leaders at all levels."

—**OMAR ISHRAK**, Chairman and CEO, Medtronic

"Govindarajan provides a winning combination of strategic insights and actionable steps designed to help virtually any business or organization build a better future."

—**AJAY BANGA**, President and CEO, MasterCard

"At PepsiCo, we practice what Govindarajan preaches."

—**INDRA K. NOOYI**, former Chairman and CEO, PepsiCo

"This book is worth reading more than once; I highly recommend it."

—**SAMUEL R. ALLEN**, Chairman and former CEO, Deere & Company

"It's refreshing to read *The Three-Box Solution* because of both its relevance and its simplicity. As you read, you connect with events in your own journey as you grapple simultaneously with ideas such as learning from the past, living in the present, and dreaming about the future. The simplicity of Govindarajan's model, like all great ideas, triggers you to think, 'Hey, why did I not think about it this way?' I recommend this book and its approach to both current and aspiring CEOs. Business schools will also find this approach worthy of teaching, and chief strategy officers will find it most useful."

—**BHASKAR BHAT**, former Managing Director, Titan Company

"*The Three-Box Solution* brilliantly tackles the challenges of a successful company to continually drive the linear innovation essential for today's operational excellence while nurturing the nonlinear innovation necessary to create the company's future."

—**GIOVANNI CAFORIO, MD**, Chairman and CEO, Bristol-Myers Squibb

"*The Three-Box Solution* is essential reading for any senior executive leading a successful company with a proud history. Govindarajan gives a clear path for how to create the environment and culture within a company to foster innovation that will make a difference in ensuring a bright future for an organization.

—**MARC N. CASPER**, President and CEO, Thermo Fisher Scientific

"In *The Three-Box Solution*, Govindarajan offers a compelling framework for driving innovation while delivering current goals, without the constraints of past successes and failures. With powerful, international examples, he offers a clear guide to creating the sustainable innovation culture needed to stay ahead."

—**IAN COOK**, Executive Chairman, former President and CEO, Colgate-Palmolive

"What a compelling piece of work—and its genius is in its simplicity. Leaders at all levels of the organization should find the three-box model for innovation a how-to manual for success."

—**ALEXANDER M. CUTLER**, former Chairman and CEO, Eaton Corporation

"*The Three-Box Solution* is an extremely stimulating, encouraging, valuable, and enjoyable read."

—**STUART FLETCHER**, former CEO, Bupa

"In *The Three-Box Solution*, Govindarajan concisely and bravely distills key insights applicable across varied industries and provides practical take-aways to facilitate execution. The book is a must-read for any manager who values courageous leadership, adaptability, and foresight."

—**BRIAN D. GOLDNER**, Chairman and CEO, Hasbro

"In today's world, organizations need to continuously innovate and demonstrate a high degree of learning ability to stay relevant and ahead of the competition. Through real-life cases and simple frameworks, Govindarajan provides insight and guidance on how leaders can prime organizations for the future while balancing the priorities of the present. *The Three-Box Solution* is a must-read for leaders at all levels."

—**N. R. NARAYANA MURTHY**, cofounder, Infosys

"The three-box approach is a pragmatic way to think through and balance the needs of existing business while crafting a future . . . Essentially, in today's business environment, leaders are required to run both a sprint and a marathon at the same time."

—**ABIDALI Z. NEEMUCHWALA, CEO** and Managing Director, Wipro Limited

"*The Three-Box Solution* offers a sound, strategic approach to ensuring that Caterpillar's long history of innovation—developing, designing, and manufacturing the machines and engines our customers want and need—continues."

—**DOUG OBERHELMAN**, former Chairman and CEO, Caterpillar

# THE
# THREE-BOX SOLUTION
# PLAYBOOK

Vijay Govindarajan
Manish Tangri

# THE

# THREE
# SOLUTION
# BOX
# PLAYBOOK

## Tools and Tactics for Creating
## Your Company's Strategy

HARVARD BUSINESS REVIEW PRESS
BOSTON, MASSACHUSETTS

**HBR Press Quantity Sales Discounts**

Harvard Business Review Press titles are available at significant quantity discounts when purchased in bulk for client gifts, sales promotions, and premiums. Special editions, including books with corporate logos, customized covers, and letters from the company or CEO printed in the front matter, as well as excerpts of existing books, can also be created in large quantities for special needs.

For details and discount information for both print and ebook formats, contact booksales@harvardbusiness.org, tel. 800-988-0886, or www.hbr.org/bulksales.

Printed in the United States of America

10 9 8 7 6 5 4 3 2 1

The web addresses referenced in this book were live and correct at the time of the book's publication but may be subject to change.

Library of Congress Cataloguing-in-Publication is forthcoming.

ISBN: 978-1-63369-830-7
eISBN: 978-1-63369-831-4

The paper used in this publication meets the requirements of the American National Standard for Permanence of Paper for Publications and Documents in Libraries and Archives Z39.48-1992.

*To my grandfather Tagore Thatha*
*who invested countless hours in my education*
*to guide—and secure—my future.*
*And to my granddaughter Meera Govinda*
*Stepenski, my hope for the future.*

—VG

*To my parents—V. K. Tangri and Asha Tangri:*
*Who are my teachers, my cheerleaders, my backbone,*
*Who have always been, whatever the*
*weather, my healing stone.*
*May we manage the present, being peaceful in the now,*
*May we selectively forget the past, the why and the how,*
*May we create the future, that makes us feel wow!*
*May we enjoy the journey to get to*
*whatever we've sought,*
*May we learn through our experiments,*
*be happy, no matter what,*
*May we share with others the good*
*we are fortunate to have got.*

—MANISH TANGRI

# CONTENTS

# THE
# THREE-BOX SOLUTION
# PLAYBOOK

# INTRODUCTION

For more than thirty-five years, one of us (VG) has taught, written about, and consulted on the challenges of building a sustainable business by establishing disciplines that enable a continuously revitalized future. I learned that the main impediments to achieving such a future are often the all-consuming demands of the current core business. The work of the present thus drains energy, organizational attention, and investment from the kinds of breakthrough innovations that fuel new business opportunities. The stress from these everyday demands of the core business is a common ailment that greatly endangers many, if not most, enterprises.

Over these three-plus decades, I studied numerous strategy failures and a smaller number of inspiring recoveries and outright successes. From my observations, I distilled a framework that shows how businesses and their people can take concerted action in three time horizons at once:

**Box 1:** executing the present core business at peak efficiency

**Box 2:** avoiding the inhibiting traps of past success

**Box 3:** building a future day by day through breakthrough innovations

I wrote about this framework in the Harvard Business Review Press book titled *The Three-Box Solution: A Strategy for Leading Innovation.* In it, I describe how foresightful, disciplined businesses have mastered each of the three boxes and built a balanced portfolio of solutions that answer the challenges of ongoing self-renewal.

My coauthor, Manish Tangri, and I present *The Three-Box Solution Playbook* to help companies apply these ideas to drive business-model innovation (Box 3) and growth. Manish has spent more than fifteen years executing entrepreneurial innovation activities in *Fortune* 500 organizations such as Microsoft and Intel. His growth-focused experiences have spanned various corporate innovation life cycles: building new businesses organically; accessing innovation competencies through acquisitions, equity investments, or partnerships; and realigning efforts through divestures or shutdowns. These experiences, which include recognizing external trends and nonlinear shifts and amplifying them so that organizations can effectively create their future, were critical in developing this playbook.

Together, through this playbook, we'll provide a *scalable and repeatable* process for creating your future while managing the present.

## The Organization of the Playbook

We've organized *The Three-Box Solution Playbook* into three parts—ideation, incubation, and scale. These three parts mirror the innovation process that we call Box 3. Further exploring these ideas, chapters 1–9 in the book include three sections:

The first section describes the key concepts, terminology, and building blocks of the three-box framework. It often uses examples from various companies to prepare the reader for each section's exercises.

Process:  In this section, we describe each section's relevant exercises and how they relate to the innovation process. We break them into sequential steps where applicable, and share practical tips based on our field experience. Please see *The Three-Box Solution Playbook Toolkit* for editable templates, exercises, and tools to support your three-box journey.

**Ideas in Practice:** Here we provide examples from companies that elucidate the process you'll conduct within your own company.

As an in-depth case study, throughout the book we use the example of the New York Times Company, which started a Box 3 experiment called New York Times Digital (NYTD) in 1995 in response to the emergence of the internet. While there certainly may be examples of other companies that have strategically reinvented business models to future-proof their growth and leadership, we like NYTD for several reasons. First, it is an easy-to-follow story. Also, the evolution of NYTD during 1995–2019 provides several teachable moments for applying the three-box framework. Second, the newspaper industry has gone through turbulent times in the last two decades. Third, NYTD is a great example to drive home the central point of the three-box solution: the idea that the *future is now*. No doubt the world will change rapidly in the future. To ensure their ability to thrive in the future, companies need to prepare now. They must think "future-back" but move from "current-forward."

In addition to the in-depth New York Times Company example, we provide breadth through other examples. Thus, we cover how the three-box framework tools apply in different industries, companies, and environments.

## How This Playbook Complements
## *The Three-Box Solution*

*The Three-Box Solution* and this playbook are highly integrated. *The Three-Box Solution* introduces the framework as well as its significance and motivates organizations to balance all three boxes to lead innovation.

*The Three-Box Solution Playbook* provides a practitioner's perspective, along with field-tested tools and methodologies that organizations can systematically apply to drive Box 3 innovations.

Because Box 3 innovation is a matter of changing business processes, mind-sets, and culture, it is accomplished most efficiently when it doesn't simply trickle down from the top. This playbook can serve as a force multiplier. The more managers in your organization who have learned to use the methodologies and tools in the playbook, the more likely change will happen faster and with less of the usual friction.

# 1

# GETTING STARTED

Strategy, for any organization, is about leadership in the future. Just because your organization is a leader today does not mean it will be a leader in the future. For every industry, the only constant is *change*. Therefore, to earn its leadership in the future, your organization must adapt to change. This is what we call innovation.

Think about all the projects your organization is executing today. How many of them will ensure that you are a leader in the future? One way to answer this question is by putting all the projects your organization is executing into three boxes:

**Box 1: Manage the present.** This box includes projects that are about improving the efficiency of your current business model—the customers you serve today, the value you offer to those customers, and the way you deliver that value. It includes product as well as process innovations, all within the frame of the current business model. We call Box 1 the *performance engine*.

**Box 2: Selectively forget the past.** This box includes two categories. First, an organization needs to identify and divest businesses that do not fit its vision for the future. Second, it must abandon the practices, ideas, and attitudes that are no longer relevant in a changed environment and that would otherwise interfere with a focus on the future.

**Box 3: Create the future.**  This box includes projects that will drive innovations to respond to such developments as technological disruptions, customer discontinuities, nontraditional competitors, and regulatory changes. Such projects may require the creation of new business models outside your organization's current Box 1 business model.

Boxes 1 and 2 are as important as Box 3—and you'll need to balance all three boxes to succeed and grow. However, with the increasing rate of change—technological discontinuities, opportunities to convert non-consumers to consumers, nontraditional competitors, and regulatory changes—many leaders find themselves at a crossroads to transform themselves and build new growth engines. To do this, you'll need to create new business models and other innovations. This tall order requires you to overcome organizational inertia, make uncertain bets, manage trade-offs, address conflicts, and, most importantly, foster a healthy partnership between the new businesses and the core businesses.

In other words, you need to pursue and execute on Box 3 ideas. That's our mission for this book—to help you do exactly that—while also helping you to manage the present and forget the things that could hold you back from pursuing the future.

## A Deeper Dive into Box 3

Box 3 innovations are nonlinear. They create new business models by dramatically (1) redefining your set of customers, (2) reinventing the value you offer them, or (3) redesigning the end-to-end value chain architecture by which you deliver that value. For example, a business school's

# THE THREE BOXES OF THE NEW YORK TIMES COMPANY

In 1995, the New York Times Company's business model was the publication of a print edition of the newspaper that served two sets of customers: highly educated readers and *Fortune* 500 companies that advertised in the newspaper to reach these influential readers. Its value proposition was premium content created by numerous Pulitzer Prize–winning journalists. The value chain architecture included the printing presses and the distribution infrastructure. Here's how company executives could have done the three-box exercise:

> **BOX 1: MANAGE THE PRESENT.** The paper's Box 1 projects included both process innovation projects and product innovation initiatives within the bounds of its current business model. For instance, in 1994 the newspaper initiated a pagination program that enabled editors to electronically design a newspaper page, including news text, graphics, and ads, thereby avoiding part or all of the manual pasteup of the various elements on a page. This change was a Box 1 process innovation. Adding a new section in the newspaper would have been a Box 1 product innovation within the company's current business model.

> **BOX 2: SELECTIVELY FORGET THE PAST.** In 2001, the New York Times Company sold its magazine group segment, which consisted of golf properties, such as *Golf Digest*, *Golf Digest Woman*, *Golf World*, and *Golf World Business*. This Box 2 move freed up resources to shape Box 3.

> **BOX 3: CREATE THE FUTURE.** Betting on the emergence of the internet as a technological disruption, the New York Times Company embarked on a Box 3 innovation project—internet media—called New York Times Digital (NYTD) in 1995. Unlike the Box 1 business model, NYTD's business model was to provide an online product and distribution channel. Should the internet grow into something big, Box 3 was how the company would earn its leadership in the future.

For the New York Times Company to build NYTD, it also had to forget the Box 1 definition of one set of its customers, the highly educated readers. It had to forget that news was created in daily cycles and that Pulitzer Prize–winning journalists were its most critical capabilities. For publishing news online, it had to abandon the printing presses. Yet, these aspects were critical to maintain Box 1 leadership.

move to offer an MBA through entirely online channels would be a non-linear innovation. It would serve a broader customer base and democratize access to high-level intellectual content while delivering the product in a fundamentally different way. Let's look at some more examples.

## Redefining Your Set of Customers

In the late 1970s, when Xerox was the market leader in selling big copiers to corporations, Canon successfully designed personal copiers at a price point significantly below Xerox's big copiers to appeal to a new set of customers: small businesses and individuals. At that time, Canon's personal copiers made 8 to 10 copies per minute and ranged in price from $700 to $1,200. In contrast, Xerox's high-speed machines made 90 to 120 copies per minute and had a price range of $80,000 to $129,000.

## Reinventing the Value You Offer Customers

Tetra Pak, a Swedish multinational, was in the business of packaging for liquid food items. Unlike traditional players that offered containers to customers, Tetra Pak changed the value proposition by offering total systems: filling equipment, packaging materials, and distribution equipment, such as conveyers, tray packers, and film wrappers. Customer value was transformed from the traditional model, namely, liquids poured into containers, to Tetra Pak's model, that is, containers made at the point where beverages were ready to be packed.

## Redesigning the Value Chain Architecture

The traditional value chain in the personal computer industry used to be categorized as *build-to-stock*, where PC manufacturers designed and manufactured several components, assembled them with preset options, and warehoused them. These assembled computers were then sent to specialized computer retailers, resellers, and other intermediaries who eventually got the PCs into the customers' hands. Dell dramatically redefined this value chain by creating the *build-to-order* model. It outsourced components to component suppliers, used its telephone network and online methods to get a customized configuration requirement from customers, assembled the components, and delivered the final product to customers.

As you'll see, Box 3 innovations are about closing what we call the possibility gap. This is the difference between the growth ambition of the company and what it can actually achieve by increasing the performance (the performance gap) of its core Box 1 business. Unlike Box 1 innovations, which are linear and incremental—that is, they seek to fill a performance gap between one's current revenue and growth goals—Box 3 innovations create the future by adding new growth through radical changes in one or more of the aforementioned business model constituents.

## The Box 3 Journey

The radical approach represented by Box 3 requires a more creative and iterative process if it is to succeed. This process involves three stages, all of which we'll cover in detail throughout this book (figure 1-1).

Ideation:  At the ideation stage, a team uses *weak signals* from within its industry to imagine the industry's future and generates nonlinear ideas by redefining one or more of the three aforementioned attributes—customer, value proposition, and value chain. These Box 3 ideas are then tested for attractiveness and strategic fit and, hence, as worthwhile ideas to incubate. Part 1 of this playbook is about ideation.

Incubation:  At the incubation stage, your team tests critical assumptions about a Box 3 idea. For example, will customers be

FIGURE 1-1

**Box 3 innovation journey**

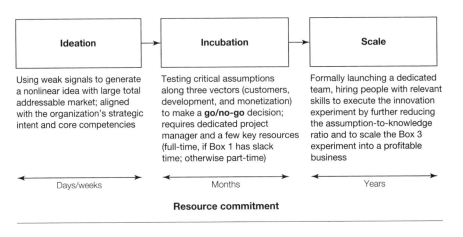

interested in the offering? Can we build the offering? And if we do, can we make money? With reasonable confidence along these three dimensions, the idea can formally be moved to the scale phase. Part 2 of this book discusses incubation.

**Scale:** In this phase, your company constructs a dedicated team and doing innovation execution, a way to implement Box 3—different from Box 1—as an experiment. Ultimately, scaling is what gets Box 3 to deliver profits back to the company. Part 3 in this book guides businesses in how they can take their innovations to a successful level of growth.

## Major Barriers to Box 3 Innovations

Box 3 innovation is difficult. As you make your way through the ideation, incubation, and scaling phases of Box 3, several traps lie in wait to undermine your efforts:

**Complacency trap:** The more a firm succeeds in the Box 1 performance engine, the more it views success as a validation of the past. The complacency trap conditions a business to suppose that success in the future requires doing nothing more than what the business has done in the past.

**Competency trap:** Favorable results from current competencies encourage an organization to invest more in those competencies, providing little incentive for the organization to invest in new competencies. In established companies built around a spectacular success, such as IBM, with its industry-defining mainframe computers, business leaders naturally want to create a workforce whose skills dominantly reflect the legacy success. But reliance on a single, established competency is a trap.

**Cannibalization trap:** This trap persuades leaders that new business models based on nonlinear ideas will jeopardize the firm's present prosperity. So, like antibodies attacking an invading virus, they protect the Box 1 business by resisting ideas that don't conform to the models of the past.

Box 3 innovation by its very nature carries a high execution risk. Leaders misjudge the Box 1 risk of obsolescence to be much lower than the Box 3 execution risk. This outlook is similar to knowing you must commit to daily exercise for long-term health while the disadvantages of *not* exercising are so minuscule on a daily basis that they go unnoticed. Only in the long term will the accumulated problems show up. Additionally, organizations are often paralyzed by the fear of failure when trying something new.

Box 3 innovation requires a change in mind-set for established organizations because they are used to predictable processes that yield predictable results, and the managers in core businesses are held accountable for results. Also, during the execution of a Box 3 idea, there will invariably be natural conflicts, not because Box 1 is resistant to change but because Box 1 and Box 3 have different jobs to do despite competing over resources, time horizons, and overlapping customers. These are very challenging issues, and to solve them, you *must bring the organization along.*

# PROCESS

Before jumping into Box 3 innovations in earnest, you'll want to step back and assess your company. What is its primary business model? How large is your growth gap? Answers to these questions, and understanding the current direction and capabilities of your company, will help you answer the most important question of all: Why do you need to pursue Box 3 innovations?

## Assessing Your Organization's Primary Business Model

Your primary business model is Box 1. Ask yourself these questions to assess its scope. Doing so will help you internalize the concept of a business model and will provide a useful baseline against which you can contrast other business models and through which you can ultimately discover new ones.

1. Who is your customer?

_____

_____

_____

_____

2. What value are you offering to your customer?

_____

_____

_____

_____

3. How have you designed the value chain to deliver that value to your customer?

_____

_____

_____

_____

4. What competencies are required to deliver that value?

_____

_____

_____

_____

5. Who are your competitors?

_____

_____

_____

_____

6. What are the current revenues and profits from your Box 1 projects?

_____

_____

_____

_____

## Assessing Your Organization's Ambition and Box 1 Leftover Growth

Next, estimate how much growth you can expect from your Box 1 business (the *performance gap*) in a given time frame and your organization's growth ambitions during the same time frame, and then compare the two.

1. What is your ambition for the revenue your organization will bring five years from now?

   _____

   _____

   _____

   _____

   _____

   _____

2. How large is your performance gap? What are the likely revenues from your Box 1 projects in five years? (In other words, how much growth is left in Box 1 to achieve your organization's revenue ambition?)

   _____

   _____

   _____

   _____

   _____

   _____

3. How large is your possibility gap? That is, how great is the difference between your ambition and your performance gap?

## Explaining Why Box 3 Is Needed

Rarely is your company's growth ambition lower than Box 1's expected growth rate (the performance gap). Therefore, you must initiate Box 3 breakthrough innovations to close the possibility gap.

There are many examples of companies that have completely disappeared when confronted by a disruptive technology. For instance, Blockbuster, a provider of in-home rental and retail sales of movies and game entertainment, employed more than eighty-four thousand people worldwide at its peak in 2004.[1] However, the company was unable to cope with nonlinear innovations, such as mail-order service, automated kiosks, and on-demand services, from companies like Netflix and Redbox. It eventually filed for bankruptcy in 2010.

While there are other examples like Blockbuster, we recommend you *resist* the temptation to jump to the doomsday narrative—that is, "If we don't invest in Box 3 innovation, we will be disrupted and reach a fate similar to Blockbuster's." Such a narrative pits Box 3 against Box 1 and minimizes Box 1's importance.

Your leadership team needs to form a narrative for pursuing Box 3 initiatives as opportunities to grow your company, as opposed to protecting against complete annihilation of Box 1. Let's look at the following reasons for pursuing both Boxes 1 and 3 for growth ambitions and some examples of companies that are doing just that.

## When Box 1 Is Insufficient

Sometimes, Box 1 alone is insufficient to achieve a company's ambition and investors' growth expectations. There are several reasons that a company needs to pursue Box 3 in addition to Box 1:

- **Our company needs a Box 3 leveraged bet to drive additional growth.** Nvidia is a visual- and accelerated-computing company that develops graphics processing units for use in PCs, mobile devices, and supercomputers. With one architecture across various large markets, the company enjoys immense leverage. Nvidia's Box 1 has been serving graphics chips in the gaming market. Nonlinear Box 3 innovations in the last few years have focused on serving new customers in data centers with new value: deep-learning accelerators to speed up artificial-intelligence computations. In its second fiscal quarter 2018 results, reported in August 2018, Nvidia's gaming revenue grew 52 percent year over year; data-center revenue grew 83 percent year over year.[2]

- **Our company needs higher-risk, high-growth Box 3 projects to drive additional growth.** Google, the world's largest search engine provider, invested in a Box 3 initiative in the autonomous-driving space. In 2016, it spun out Waymo as a separate company. Waymo is widely recognized as one of the leaders in autonomous driving.

- **Our company's Box 1 is firing on all cylinders today, but Box 1 growth is likely to slow or stagnate in the near future.** Over the last few years, Walmart, one of the largest retailers in the world, has been steadily investing in Box 3 online retail and e-commerce initiatives to drive additional growth. Furthermore, in May 2018, Walmart rolled out Jetblack, a chat-based personal shopping service targeting time-strapped mothers in New York City.[3] Jetblack allows members to text when they run out of cereal or need a last-minute gift recommendation, for example, and provides same- or next-day delivery with free returns.

- **Our Box 1 is in a decline or, worse, is a burning platform.** Electrolux was in decline in 2002. The European manufacturer of household appliances served midrange customers, but people's priorities were changing. Customers were gravitating to either the low end of the market or the premium end. As a result, the CEO took on a multiyear Box 3 initiative to target premium customers by building new competencies, such as customer insight teams and industrial design.

- **Our Box 1 simply cannot address the emerging industry dynamics, because of current business-model limitations.** In 2002, Timberland was competing in the footwear industry, where the fast creation of new subcategories was the norm. The company churned out new offerings twice a year, but when the company recognized a trend toward specialty shoes, Box 1 processes were inadequate to address it. Timberland embarked on a Box 3 project that would be free from the month-to-month pressures of Box 1. The company ultimately created specialty shoes for trail runners, who had different needs from road runners. People who ran on the road cared most about minimizing the strain on joints, whereas trail runners wanted to avoid falling. It took Timberland five years to launch the new offering for trail runners.

- **Newer opportunities, such as emerging markets, require a Box 3 move.**
  To target nonconsumers at the bottom of the pyramid in India,
  General Electric made a Box 3 move to completely reimagine its
  electrocardiogram (ECG) machines and make them ultra-low-
  cost, portable, and battery-operable.

## When Box 3 Innovation Makes Better Sense Than Box 1 Innovation

Sometimes, innovation is possible in both Box 1 and Box 3 projects. But
for the following reasons, good strategy favors Box 3.

- **In our investment-constrained environment, Box 3 innovation is cheaper
  than Box 1.** In 2002, Lucent Technologies, a network equipment
  business, was hit hard by the dot-com bust. Technological
  innovation was very much embedded in Lucent's DNA. And
  although the company had forecast revenues of $40 billion during
  the boom, reality was that its revenues were under $10 billion.
  In the battle for survival, Lucent was forced to consider newer
  models of growth. The services market seemed attractive since
  the company already had a services team to repair and maintain the equipment constituting its core business. Expanding the
  team beyond Lucent switches to the entire telecom network was
  a cheaper Box 3 move than were incremental investments in new
  technologies in Box 1.

- **We have a Box 1 that limits Box 3 from taking shape and is taking the business in the wrong direction.** Tata Consultancy Services (TCS), one
  of India's largest information technology (IT) services company,
  had become successful in the thriving sector of offshore call centers at the start of the millennium. Despite the business's growth,
  TCS decided to discontinue its call-center service after a few
  years. Experience showed that the average tenure of a call-center

operator ranged from three months to a year, according to TCS's former CEO Subramaniam Ramadorai. This high workforce churn, with as many as a half million workers cycling through the company annually, caused an intense drain on management energy. Closing down the call-center service allowed TCS to free up resources for Box 3.

Now that you've laid the groundwork, articulate precisely why you need Box 3 (fill in the following statement). This critical step helps all key stakeholders see the value of, and urgency for, Box 3 and recognize that Box 1 is also an integral part of the answer to future growth.

Our company needs Box 3 innovation now because . . .

# Creating an Inventory of Box 3 Projects

Finally, create a list of Box 3 projects already under way in your organization, and identify their stage (ideation, incubation, scale). For each Box 3, ensure that there is a nonlinear difference, relative to Box 1, across one or more of the three dimensions: customer, value proposition, and value chain. That is, a Box 3 project is not an incrementally larger, faster, or better version of a Box 1 project but rather is a significantly new take on at least one of the three dimensions.

**Box 3 project:**

**Stage:**

| Dimension | Short description | Nonlinear difference between Box 3 and Box 1? (Yes/No) |
|---|---|---|
| Customer | | |
| Value proposition | | |
| Value chain | | |

After completing the application exercises, review "The Path Ahead" table at the end of this chapter to map your next step, depending on where you are in your Box 3 journey. In each chapter, we will guide you through the relevant concepts, processes, and exercises.

# IDEAS IN PRACTICE

In the mid-1990s, as the newspaper industry was facing challenges from the internet, the New York Times Company (NYTimes) had to make several tough strategic decisions. These decisions focused on the creation of a Box 3 innovation, the digital product NYTD, which has been very successful. Even though one-fifth of the newspapers in the United States have shut down in the last fifteen years—roughly more than eighteen hundred newspapers since 2004—the New York Times Company has been more successful.[4] It more than doubled its market cap between March 1995 and November 2019, with a meaningful revenue contribution from digital-only subscriptions.[5] Let's wind back the clock and imagine how the Times tried to develop its future path.

## The Box 1 Business Model of the NYTimes

In 1995, the business model of the NYTimes could have been described as follows:

**Customers:** The company had two primary customers: the highly educated readers of the printed paper and the *Fortune* 500 companies that advertised in the printed newspaper.

**Value offering:** The NYTimes offered premium content at a premium price for subscriptions and especially for advertising.

**Value chain:** The chain that delivered value to its customers had several components. The company purchased 276,000 metric tons of newsprint through long-term contracts from its suppliers. Pulitzer Prize–winning journalists gathered the facts and wrote the news articles. The articles were processed through electronic news-editing terminals and sent to high-resolution image setters. The papers were printed in a New York

City production facility and were produced and distributed to individual customers by a facility in Edison, New Jersey. City and Suburban Delivery Systems, a company-owned wholesale distributor, delivered the product to retail outlets.

**Competencies required to deliver value:**  Among the capabilities necessary for delivering value to NYTimes customers were the top-notch journalists who, by 2019, have delivered seventy-nine Pulitzer Prizes to the newspaper; the extensive printing, production, and distribution facilities. Finally, there were the 12,300 full-time employees. Overall, 3,600 of these employees were represented by sixteen unions; there were collective bargaining agreements with six production unions and six non-production unions.

**Competitors:**  Competing with the NYTimes were newspapers of general circulation and, to varying degrees, national publications such as the *Wall Street Journal* and *USA Today.*

**Revenues and profits or operating margin:**  In 1995, the company had approximately $2.1 billion in annual revenues; $208 million in operating profit, with a 10 percent operating margin.

## The Possibility Gap of the NYTimes

Next, the NYTimes assessed its possibility gap, which eventually would be serviced by Box 3 projects. To make this assessment, the company looked at its revenue ambition for the next five years. Its revenue had grown at a compound annual growth rate (CAGR) of 5.8 percent over the past five years. Let's assume the company's growth ambition was 8 percent CAGR over the next five years, to a total revenue of approximately $3.5 billion. It then would have to figure how much growth remained in its Box 1 to reach this five-year ambition. The estimated necessary growth constituted the company's performance gap.

Box 1 revenue was expected to grow at a CAGR of 4.9 percent (performance gap) over the next five or six years, to about $2.8 billion in 2001. The possibility gap was 3.1 percent (8 percent growth ambition minus the 4.9 percent leftover growth for Box 1).

## The Need for a Box 3 Innovation

Building on the preceding information, how did the NYTimes articulate its need for a Box 3 innovation? The company understood that its Box 1 growth was slowing. The newspaper's circulation had been declining by more than twenty thousand copies per year since 1993. With newsprint prices rising significantly and forecast to grow by more than $76 million by the end of 1995, the company had to offset the cost by selling more advertising and implementing cost controls. The company's possibility gap was 3.1 percent. Thus, the NYTimes needed to bet on a higher-growth and maybe higher-risk Box 3 that was in line with the future of the industry as a new source of revenue.

Considering the emergence of the internet, the NYTimes leaders knew they had to explore newer ways to reach their readers and provide better ways for their advertisers to target those readers. In fact, the previous year, the NYTimes had experimented with an online service, called @times, which shared information from the *New York Times* on America Online (AOL). The trial had been widely successful, as @times was then one of AOL's most frequently accessed services. The leaders reasoned that if the internet took off, it could be big and the NYTimes could lead rather than follow this trend.

## The Box 3 Idea of the NYTimes

The NYTimes leaders came up with the idea of creating a digital version of the newspaper. This was a Box 3 idea. It redefined not only the consumer set that the company was targeting but also the value proposition and the way that value was delivered to the consumers.

| Dimension | Short description | Nonlinear difference between Box 3 and Box 1? (Yes/No) |
|---|---|---|
| Customer | General consumer worldwide, not just limited to the United States | Yes |
| Value proposition | Nonpremium content at low cost, with some paid premium content | Yes |
| Value chain | Produced and distributed online | Yes |

## The Path Ahead

Depending on where your organization stands with its Box 3 development, you will want to start moving forward at the appropriate place. The following table shows the most pertinent chapters for you to consult next for your Box 3 challenges:

| Your present status | Book segments to consult |
|---|---|
| You have no Box 3 ideas; you are starting from scratch. | Chapters 2-5 |
| You don't have enough Box 3 ideas. | Chapters 2-5 |
| You have a Box 3 but are not sure it is the right one. | Chapters 2, 3, 4, and "Selecting Ideas" section of Chapter 5 |
| You have a Box 3 but have not yet made a go/no-go decision. | Chapter 6 |
| You have a Box 3 but are still trying to determine product-market fit. | Chapter 6 |
| You have a Box 3 but are not executing it fast enough. | Chapters 7-9 |
| You have a Box 3 but are running into conflicts with Box 1. | Chapter 8 |
| You have a Box 3 but are not achieving results. | Chapter 9 |

PART
ONE

# IDEATION

n the next four chapters, we'll introduce the methodology you need for developing Box 3 ideas. In chapter 2, you will identify market discontinuities through weak signals, which will help you imagine the future of your industry and think about nonlinear changes you must pay attention to.

Chapters 3 and 4 discuss the importance of understanding your organization's strategic intent and core competencies. This understanding will help you pick which Box 3 ideas, among various potential options, are the best fit for your company or organization.

In chapter 5, with the backdrop of nonlinear changes, strategic intent, and core competencies, you will generate a list of Box 3 ideas and prune the list to ultimately pick the top Box 3 idea.

Teams often find ideation to be one of the most enjoyable parts of the innovation journey, having fun working together and building on each other's ideas. We hope you and your team will enjoy the journey.

# 2

# GATHERING WEAK SIGNALS

To identify future market discontinuities, you must gather *weak signals*—emergent changes to technology, culture, markets, the economy, consumer tastes and behavior, and demographics. As the name suggests, weak signals are hard to evaluate because they are incomplete, unsettled, and unclear. But they are the raw material for making hypotheses about nonlinear changes in the future. These changes feed into generating Box 3 ideas that usually lie at the intersection of multiple market discontinuities.

An understanding of weak signals starts with three basic questions:

1. What factors and conditions contribute to the success of our current business model?

2. Which of these factors might change over time—or are changing already—thus putting current success at risk?

3. How can we prepare for these possible changes to cushion or even exploit their impact?

Proactively looking for weak signals will help you imagine the future of your industry. Consider how the following conditions might create these weak signals. Ask yourself questions about these situations, and then see how some companies have taken advantage of the weak signals.

## Customer Discontinuities

Who will be your customers in the future? What priorities will they have? A company in the search engine industry may see weak signals, such as the growing use of technology among younger children, and anticipate the need to cater to a new customer segment: kids. Kiddle, for instance, is a search engine designed specifically for kids.[1] Focusing on showing safe sites that satisfy family-friendly requirements, it provides up to three results that are specifically written for kids and another one to three results that are not written for kids but are handpicked by the editors to ensure that the material is easy to understand. The results are shown with large thumbnails to make them easy to see and in fonts that are easier for kids to read.

In a similar vein, since 2018 Facebook has been targeting kids under thirteen with its Messenger Kids app. For a long time, social network companies, in accordance with the Children's Online Privacy Protection Act, prohibited children younger than thirteen from signing up on the network. However, in a 2017 poll conducted on behalf of Facebook and National PTA, three out of five American parents said that their children under age thirteen used messaging apps, social media, or both. Facebook's goal is to put parents at ease through its design of full parental controls, such as requiring parents' authorization for a child to sign up and to add each new contact. Whether the approach is successful, given the huge uproar against Facebook, remains to be seen.

## Technological Discontinuities

What disruptive technologies can open up new opportunity spaces? Illumina, a San Diego–based firm that sells genome-sequencing machines to software and services companies that analyze the data, provides a good example of disruptive technologies. In a landmark technology innovation, Illumina developed the capability to run a large number of parallel sequencing reactions on a small instrument. This capability helped dramatically drive down the cost of genome sequencing and opened up opportunities for new business models that require genomes to be sequenced.

## Nontraditional Competitors

Are today's most potent competitors likely to be the same competitors in the future? Who will you be competing against in the future? And on what basis?

Edge computing, where data processing and storage are moving closer to the device or user, is a current trend. It improves application response time. Telecommunications industry players, such as Verizon, AT&T, Sprint, and T-Mobile, are facing competition from cloud service providers, such as Google, Microsoft, and Amazon, as they all compete for the edge infrastructure play. This situation is particularly significant given that telecom players lost to technology companies in the battle for over-the-top (OTT) services—voice, messaging, and video. OTT players, such as Apple's FaceTime, Google Hangouts, Microsoft's Skype, Tencent QQ, and Facebook's WhatsApp, are offering services that were a staple domain of the traditional telecom companies. If the telecom industry just stands still, it will be changed forever in the next ten-plus years.

## HASBRO, A COMPANY THAT RECOGNIZED AND ADDRESSED MULTIPLE WEAK SIGNALS

Starting in the mid-1990s, Hasbro, manufacturer of popular toys (including G.I. Joe and My Little Pony) and board games (such as Monopoly), transformed itself from a product company to a "branded play" company by recognizing several weak signals. The company noted the rise of PCs and the debut of Atari's video gaming system, a falling birth rate in the United States, rising ethnic diversity, and an increasing number of two-income households.

With little presence in emerging markets in 2000, Hasbro subsequently grew to earn 50 percent of revenues from non-US markets, including significant revenues from emerging markets. The company has increased its emphasis on digital gaming. Hasbro's teams have leveraged core brands, such as Transformers, across multiple platforms—toys, movies, television, and the internet (including social media). In 2000, Hasbro's top eight brands delivered 20 percent of total revenues; as of 2018, they accounted for over 50 percent.

### New Distribution Channels

Will there be fundamental changes in your go-to-market approach in the future? Consider, Amazon, which already partners with FedEx and UPS for delivery. But looking further into the future, Amazon is also exploring new ways to deliver packages by drones, given that more than 80 percent of its packages weigh less than five pounds.[2]

### Regulatory Changes

What are some key regulatory changes that could significantly affect the future of your company and how it responds to customers, competitors, and partners? Regulatory changes, such as the Affordable Care Act that

Barack Obama signed into law in 2010 to bring insurance to uninsured individuals, radically overhauled the US individual health-insurance industry. With more than 20 million people added to the population that already had medical insurance coverage, and with the abolishment of the preexisting-conditions restriction, the risk pools for health-plan populations dramatically changed. Requirements to cover preventive services, such as cancer screening and immunizations, led insurers to invest in scale. Major players embarked on mergers to stabilize the costs of operating health-care coverage. Health-care regulations will continue to evolve in the future, presenting new opportunities as well as challenges.

# PROCESS

Gathering weak signals requires several steps. Among other steps, you must form a diverse team to capture a variety of viewpoints and to conduct research.

## The Team

People who are good at recognizing weak signals don't wear blinders. Their work contains a feedback loop through which they see and "feel" such signals. Younger people in the company, in terms of both rank and years of service, who have not grown accustomed to seeing things a certain way, are great team members.

Other good candidates are individuals who excel at observing schema-breaking changes. They might encounter these anomalies through their work on new technologies or through their interactions with universities or other environments. These individuals may also observe weak signals when they work on customers' problems at their sites or collaborate with entrepreneurs. When pulling your team together, choose from the following categories to guarantee a diverse set of opinions:

- Market- and customer-centric people (e.g., product managers, salespeople, marketing personnel)

- Technologists (e.g., application engineers, systems engineers, architects)

- Business-centric people (e.g., finance and business development people)

- Industry experts (e.g., *internal*: competitor intelligence and strategic planning teams, corporate development and venture teams; *external*: ecosystem stakeholders, consultants, investment bankers, venture capitalists, market-research firms)

## The Research

How you gather these signals could vary from any of the following methods (ordered from least to most expensive):

1. Conduct primary research with key stakeholders through interviews conducted either by your own team or by an external firm; the timeline could stretch from weeks to months.

2. Organize a small, focused industry summit (around forty people), inviting internal and external stakeholders; typically, the event would range from a day to no more than a week.

3. Use software tools that run innovation contests and jam sessions to gather insights from your entire organization and more; these systems allow you to do continuous scanning throughout the year.

Whatever your research approach, you'll want to gather weak signals in the following categories as groundwork for the remainder of the ideation process:

| Category | Signal | Evidence | Signal strength (Weak/Strong) |
|---|---|---|---|
| Customer discontinuities | | | |
| Technological discontinuities | | | |
| Nontraditional competitors | | | |
| New distribution channels | | | |
| Regulatory changes | | | |

If you were a leader in the health-care industry, the weak signals you identified might have looked something like this:

**CUSTOMERS:** First, through your work identifying weak signals, you may have found that there are many nonconsumers in the health-care industry. In fact, the industry caters to only about 15 percent of the world's population; nonconsumers are 85 percent. Most of these nonconsumers reside in emerging markets. The key question to ask is, "Is there an opportunity in converting these nonconsumers to consumers?"

**DISRUPTIVE TECHNOLOGIES:** Genetic engineering can open up a variety of new opportunities if you are a pharmaceutical company.

**NONTRADITIONAL COMPETITORS:** Silicon Valley technology companies, such as Google, are entering the market because they have the technical talent to bring health care to your home—for example, through teleconferencing technologies.

**DISTRIBUTION CHANNELS:** As described above, mobile technologies can disrupt traditional distribution channels such as in-person visits and paper records.

**REGULATORY CHANGES:** The speed of obtaining regulatory approvals like those provided by the US Food and Drug Administration or patent protection policies could determine the country for which you design and launch products.

# IDEAS IN PRACTICE

Let's consider a global construction firm engaged in a spectrum of activities, from design to build, in the year 2014. The following chart shows how it would identify key market discontinuities and weak signals in various categories:

| Category | Signal | Evidence | Signal strength (Weak/Strong) |
|---|---|---|---|
| **Customer discontinuities** | The construction-firm customer base is declining in and around San Francisco. Demand is moving to the government as a customer. | Competitors are moving headquarters from San Francisco to near Washington, D.C., or Houston. Demand in government contracting, oil and gas services, and maintenance of nuclear facilities has been increasing over the past few years. | Strong |
| **Technological discontinuities** | New technologies—3-D printing, drones, laser scanning, remote-controlled cranes—are being used intermittently. | A Silicon Valley startup is building drones and has recently partnered with a large construction company. The startup is using drones to create high-accuracy digital maps and reduce time to completion in construction projects. More research papers on these topics are being published in top universities. | Weak |
| **Nontraditional competitors** | New entrants are attacking a higher-margin niche of data-center construction. | Demand for new data centers closer to urban areas is growing rapidly to address connectivity issues facing cloud-based applications and to address edge-computing needs of customers. A well-funded startup in Texas, with branded venture capital investors, has demonstrated a modularized colocation data center that was built in a record six months, when typical construction of a nonmodularized data center takes much longer. | Weak |
| **New distribution channels** | Consultants in premium buildings market are using embedded electronics (cameras, the Internet of Things, digital security platforms) as a differentiator. | Newer construction featuring state-of-the-art technology (cameras, sensors, digital security platforms, and the Internet of Things) is prefabricated as part of the building. Owners can charge higher rent. Two recent buildings reached less than 5 percent vacancy twice as fast as the local average. | Weak |
| **Regulatory changes** | A government initiative on standardizing and simplifying building codes has increased production and scale and has lowered costs for construction firms. | City permit departments are doing a pilot project in one county. | Weak |
| | Federal Aviation Agency regulations for flying commercial drones in construction space has been weakened. | License approval has been shortened from nine months to less than the time required to obtain a heavy-crane operator license. | Strong |

## Wrap-Up

To develop Box 3 ideas, you need to pay attention to emerging disconti-nuities in your industry or in the wider world. These sometimes-hard-to-spot changes, or weak signals, may seem subtle. But watching out for them helps you and your team think beyond Box 1.

- The first step in ideation is to identify nonlinear changes in your company's industry by becoming aware of weak signals.

- These signals may forecast the future, or they could simply be noise.

- Systematically gathering weak signals in a variety of catego-ries, through a set of inputs, helps you think more broadly and diversely.

# 3

# STRATEGIC INTENT

Now that you've gathered a number of weak signals, you need to brainstorm ideas that are the right fit for your organization. So next, we'll walk you through the shaping of your organization's strategic intent, which will provide direction for brainstorming and identifying Box 3 ideas.[1] To paraphrase the Cheshire Cat from *Alice's Adventures in Wonderland*, if you don't know where you are going, any road will take you there.

Unlike mission statements, which are sometimes generic, broad, and aspirational, a strategic intent statement must meet three criteria:

**Direction:** A strategic intent statement must galvanize your team to create the future. Direction is about the big picture, not all the steps you have to take to get there. One great example of making the big picture visual is that of Muhammad Yunus, founder of Grameen Bank, a microfinance and community development bank founded in Bangladesh. Yunus's aspiration is to eliminate poverty. Just as dinosaur museums were constructed because there are no living dinosaurs to see, Yunus's strategic intent is to create "poverty museums" after poverty, like the dinosaurs, no longer exists.

**Motivation:** A strategic intent statement must also create passion. Would employees be excited to go to work if the CEO said, "Our mission is to create shareholder wealth"? On the contrary, a statement that shows appreciation for employees' capabilities helps them feel considerable personal meaning in their work and will go far in exciting people about creating the future beyond mere financial goals.

**Challenge:** To challenge employees to do something bold, a strategic intent statement must express a sizable possibility gap. Yunus's intent to eliminate poverty meets the test of a huge possibility gap.

A strategic intent is a *choice* you make after evaluating what is changing in the world around you, what the implications of those changes

## JOHN F. KENNEDY'S MAN ON THE MOON

Let's look at a strategic intent statement that meets all three criteria. "I believe that this nation should commit itself to achieving the goal, before this decade is out, of landing a man on the moon and returning him safely to the Earth."[2] In 1961, President Kennedy excited Americans' imagination with this statement. Compare this statement with another he could have made: "We want to become aeronautical leaders in the world."

Let's test the Kennedy's man-on-the-moon statement against the three criteria:

**DIRECTION:** The statement has a great visual component. Even a five-year-old can understand what it means to go to the moon and come back.

**MOTIVATION:** The Soviet Union had already launched ahead in the space race in the 1950s. Kennedy's statement was a call to action to show superiority against the Soviet Union, igniting the aspirations of the masses.

**CHALLENGE:** Certainly, there was a huge challenge—a huge possibility gap—embedded in the man-on-the-moon statement. Nobody had ever set foot on the moon.

are for your company, and what your aspirations are for the future. Strategic intent is about thinking big, dreaming big, and having an unrealistic goal.

We create our vision by starting with the future and working backward from there; we disregard the resource scarcity of the present. Successful organizations imagine the future in bold terms. The details are not fixed, but the big picture and the direction are clear and everyone is aligned. Why do we need an unrealistic goal? As human beings, we perform according to our expectations; we rarely exceed them. People are drawn to bold and challenging goals. Deep inside, the thought of climbing a mountain uplifts us in a way that the idea of scaling a molehill does not.

If your company has to become a leader in the future, you first have to imagine the future. Articulating a strategic intent that passes the direction, motivation, and challenge criteria is an important tool—as it provides scope and anchors the company in pursuit of its goals.

## CHANGING YOUR STRATEGIC INTENT STATEMENT

Examples of companies that have changed their strategic intent statements abound. In the 1980s, for example, Hasbro's strategic intent was to be the "leading US toys and games producer." In the 1990s, the company changed its intent to be the "leading toys and games producer in the world." Over the last fifteen years, the company's quest has been to be a "leading entertainment company," resulting in its entry into movie production.[3] By evolving its strategic intent, a company like Siemens, once a manufacturer of X-ray machines, can go from being a "medical imaging company" to a "medical devices company" to, more radically, a "health-care management company." Similarly, Ford could go from a world-class automobile company to a world-class mobility company.

# PROCESS

To develop a strategic intent statement, take the following steps:

**Step 1:** Imagine the future of your industry, building on the weak-signals exercise in chapter 2, and write down what you anticipate.

_____

_____

_____

_____

**Step 2:** Assess whether your current *strategic intent*, which your organization may have set earlier, is still applicable within that future context.

_____

_____

_____

_____

If yes, test for the three criteria—direction, motivation, and challenge—and refine as needed.

| Statement | Direction (Yes/No) | Motivation (Yes/No) | Challenge (Yes/No) |
|---|---|---|---|
| | | | |

**Step 3:** If your strategic intent needs some work, divide into three teams to brainstorm three strategic intent directions. Think about what is changing the world, what those changes mean for your company, and what your company's aspirations are, given those changes.

| Statement | Notes |
|---|---|
| 1. | |
| 2. | |
| 3. | |

**Step 4:** Apply the three criteria—direction, motivation, and challenge—and assess which of the statements is the best fit for your organization.

| Statement | Direction (Yes/No) | Motivation (Yes/No) | Challenge (Yes/No) |
|---|---|---|---|
| 1. | | | |
| 2. | | | |
| 3. | | | |

**Step 5:** Test the strategic intent statement. For instance, if you radically change the customer set, value proposition, or value chain architecture, will the strategic intent endure the change? If the strategic intent statement doesn't hold, then use the following lines to refine it further, for example, to ultimately ensure that it can target not only current consumers but also nonconsumers. Otherwise, leave the lines blank.

_____

_____

_____

_____

# IDEAS IN PRACTICE

In early October 2015, the New York Times Company celebrated a remarkable achievement by clearing one million digital subscribers. What took the printed newspaper a century to achieve, the company's websites and apps attained in just five years. The bet on the weak signal generated by the internet had paid off. In five years, the company had doubled the digital-only revenues to roughly $400 million.[4]

As the company imagined the future, it released a report titled "Our Path Forward," which stated its ambition to double its digital revenues to more than $800 million by 2020. One way to achieve this goal was to double the number of engaged digital readers, who were the underpinning of the consumer and advertising revenue models.

The NYTimes realized that it needed to move from a print-era organization to a mobile-era one. Whereas the first two million subscribers, including the one million-plus newspaper subscribers, grew up with the *New York Times* spread over their kitchen tables, the next million had to be fought for and won with the *Times* on their phones. Furthermore, this goal had to be reached in an environment of relentless change in technology, consumer behavior, and business models.

The following intent statements illustrate how the NYTimes described its approach to the future:

1. The NYTimes will continue to lead the industry in creating the best original journalism and storytelling.

2. The company will transform the product experience to make the *New York Times* an even more important part of its readers' daily lives.

3. It will continue to develop new audiences and grow the *Times* as an international institution, just as the company once successfully turned a metro paper into a national one.

4. The NYTimes will improve the customer experience for its readers, enabling them to more easily form and deepen a relationship with the *New York Times.*

5. The NYTimes will continue to grow digital advertising by creating compelling integrated ad experiences that match the quality and innovation of the *New York Times.*

6. The company will continue to provide the best newspaper experience for its print readers and advertisers while carefully shifting time and energy to its digital platforms.

7. The company will organize its operations with a focus on its readers, not on legacy processes and structures.

Notice the word *readers* occurs in four of the seven bullets. The NYTimes must definitely cater to its readers, particularly as the print business declines slowly while the digital business expands rapidly and as both businesses will probably coexist beyond 2020.

When imagining the future, however, we must be open to heretofore-unimagined possibilities. In the case of the NYTimes, the company might have imagined that at some point, "readers" would consume content in other ways, such as video, and thus turn into viewers. Even from a US standpoint, 2015 was a landmark year, in which consumers spent more time consuming digital video than they did social media.[5] With the benefit of hindsight, we can see the trend has been accelerating. By January 2019, as 4G data rates dropped below $2 per month in India, the volume of video streamed on smartphones had grown tenfold. People in India are using YouTube as a search engine. They find it easier to watch something than to sift through text, making India the country with YouTube's largest audience in 2018.[6] Thus, the strategic intent statement should not be limited to "readers" but should encompass "users" or "consumers" as well.

In building its strategic intent, the NYTimes could have gone in three directions:

- Advertiser first, such as a focus on maximizing readership

- User first, such as a focus on building loyal, paying, engaged customers

- Something totally radical, such as an OTT TV provider (e.g., Sling TV)

The company decided to focus on users first, building a loyal, highly engaged, paying customer base. This decision doesn't imply that the NYTimes should give up on advertisers as a business model. But the clarity in the company's strategic intent helps its leaders understand the trade-offs when they have to make hard decisions. As a business leader, you may be tempted to say that you will focus on multiple dimensions of your business, but doing so would weaken the direction of your strategic intent statement.

We can imagine that, equipped with this backdrop, three NYTimes teams might have come up with the following strategic intent statements incorporating the *direction* test:

- The NYTimes will be the best media company on the planet, built on the most loyal consumer base.

- The NYTimes will inspire engaged consumers to lead active and ambitious lives and will do so through the best original journalism and storytelling in a digital-first world.

- Whatever the weather, whatever the platform, the NYTimes will deliver the story that illuminates consumers' minds throughout the world and throughout their lives.

As the example of the NYTimes shows, you and your team need to base your strategic intent statement on energizing your organization. The winning statement must pass the motivation and challenge tests.

You will also want to pressure-test your strategic intent to ensure that it is not too narrow; strategic intent must allow for many Box 3 ideas. For instance, does the signal of video proliferation discussed earlier get captured in the NYTimes winning strategic intent statement? For example, Google's mission statement, "To organize the world's information and make it universally accessible and useful," allows the company to pursue the direction of being in the news business. On the other hand, the NYTimes strategic intent statement doesn't capture the search business.

## Wrap-Up

Once you have gathered several weak signals, the next step in ideation is to develop a statement of strategic intent. Keep in mind these caveats when considering what constitutes a successful statement:

- Strategic intent should be considered within the context of the nonlinear changes in the industry.

- A statement of strategic intent must do three things: direct, motivate, and challenge.

- Strategic intent provides a broad direction within which Box 3 ideas can be generated.

# 4

# CORE COMPETENCIES

The next crucial step in building a Box 3 strategy is identifying your organization's core competencies—the things that separate you from your competitors. Core competencies may seem straightforward, but to correctly identify them, you need to look beyond your products, customers, physical assets, and talent. Those are capabilities and advantages. Core competencies, on the other hand, are about know-how. Always an intangible asset, core competencies are something you do, and they can never be a single skill.

For example, one of Honda's core competencies is its ability to design, engineer, and manufacture small engines. Let's assume for the sake of simplicity that Honda has one thousand engineers in its R&D lab in three underlying technologies: combustion technology, electronic controls, and microprocessor controls. Suppose you hired one thousand engineers in the same three technologies. Will you be able to match Honda's world-class capability in designing, engineering, and manufacturing small engines? The answer is no. Honda has a system, a culture, and a methodology by which these thousand engineers have learned to work together in an integrated, synergistic way over a long period. It is the company's collective and cumulative learning that you cannot replicate overnight. And not only has Honda integrated its technical skills in its R&D lab, but the company has also integrated R&D with manufacturing, so that Honda designs for manufacturing. Additionally, Honda has integrated R&D with marketing, addressing customer problems in the design.

As this example shows, core competency is an organization-level concept. Core competencies are good ways to vet ideas—and will help you determine which of several seemingly good Box 3 ideas you're better suited to take on.

# PROCESS

To figure out your company's core competencies, you must dig into why you offer better value to your customers than your competition does. Are there things that only your company can uniquely do? Or things that it can do better than everybody else? If so, what combination of skills, know-how, and intangibles constitutes your ability to do so?

List your organization's three to five key core competencies:

1. _____

_____

_____

_____

2. _____

_____

_____

_____

3. _____

_____

_____

_____

4. _____

_____

_____

_____

5. _____

_____

_____

_____

Then ask yourself the following questions, and fill in the chart that follows those questions.

**Can you exploit this competency across multiple growth platforms?** You should be able to extend your organization's core competency to create new revenue streams. For instance, Honda can apply its small-engine know-how to put a small engine in a motorcycle, an automobile, a snowblower, a power tool, and so forth.

**Can it contribute significant customer value?** Customers never see your core competency. However, they can tell you why they are buying your product. They can point to the functionalities that are relevant to them. You have to make the connection between customer benefits and the competence needed to deliver those benefits. For instance, if you buy a Honda snowblower and someone asks why you bought that brand, you probably won't respond, "Because of Honda's competence in engine technology." Instead, you might say, "When the first major snowstorm hits town and I pull out the snowblower, it starts with a roar even if it has been sitting in the garage for twelve months. The fuel efficiency is outstanding when we operate it. And it's really quiet and safe." So the question is whether the small-engine design has anything to do with the reliability of the snowblower and its performance. The answer is yes.

**Is the core competency difficult to imitate in the medium term?** Although other companies could recruit engineers to try to replicate Honda's success, they couldn't imitate Honda's world-class design capabilities within a reasonable period.

| Core competency | Growth? (Yes/No) | Customer value? (Yes/No) | Imitate? (Yes/No) |
|---|---|---|---|
| 1. | | | |
| 2. | | | |
| 3. | | | |

| Core competency | Growth? (Yes/No) | Customer value? (Yes/No) | Imitate? (Yes/No) |
|---|---|---|---|
| 4. | | | |
| 5. | | | |

The core competencies you identify must be something you do today, not a company belief from the past. In other words, be intellectually honest. Avoid assuming that the advantages that were relevant years ago are still current.

# IDEAS IN PRACTICE

User experience has long been one of Apple's most important competencies. When the iPhone debuted in 2007, its intuitive design and usability were dramatically better than competing products. It did not require reading manuals, and even young children could navigate the device. Apple has always paid attention to details, such as packaging and branding, to ensure that users have a great functional and emotional experience every time they engage with Apple products. From computers to phones to the Apple Watch, this core competency extends to all the company's products, drives significant price premiums, and was defended by Apple for years despite other companies' efforts to imitate it.

Other companies also enjoyed success by focusing on a core competency. For example, the NYTimes excelled in storytelling; before the dominance of the digital world, the company led the industry in this area of expertise. As described earlier, Canon challenged industry titan Xerox with the smaller company's expertise in miniaturizing copiers. For FedEx, the core competency was logistics in express shipping. And 3M became a world expert in adhesives and dominates its market segment.

## Wrap-Up

By taking the third step in ideation, namely, identifying your core competencies, you figure out what separates you from the competition. Keep the following observations in mind when trying to take strategic advantage of your competencies:

- Because core competencies are knowledge-based assets, they are intangible.

- Core competencies are more than just products, physical assets, or talent.

- You need to develop new core competencies to future-proof your company.

# 5

# GENERATING AND SELECTING BOX 3 IDEAS

Now that you've identified weak signals, solidified your strategic intent, and identified your organization's core competencies, you can begin brainstorming Box 3 ideas. These ideas make a nonlinear change in one or more of the following dimensions: the customer being served, the value proposition to the customer, or the value chain to deliver the value proposition. As described earlier, a Box 3 idea lies at the intersection of two or more nonlinear shifts in the industry: customer discontinuities, disruptive technologies, future competitors, distribution channels, or regulatory changes.

Your job now is to generate ideas that exploit those intersections. Then we'll show you how to prune the list. At the end of the process, you'll have selected the best Box 3 idea.

# THE LOW-COST ECG MACHINE

In the early 2000s, GE Healthcare's Box 1 business was to deliver complex, high-performance medical imaging equipment at a premium price—like $20,000 ECG machines—to premier hospitals. But it was also on the lookout for Box 3 ideas. The GE team saw two weak signals. There were many nonconsumers in rural India with limited access to health care, and several mobile and battery technologies were emerging at the time.

To flesh out their ideas, the GE team members sought to understand the unique pain points for the rural Indian consumer. These consumers, who earn around $2 a day, cannot afford to pay $200 per scan, which is the cost of scans generated by the $20,000 ECG machine. But even if customers could afford the scans, there are no hospitals with sophisticated imaging centers. Someone would have to take the $20,000 instrument, which weighs five hundred pounds, door-to-door. Furthermore, the machine only works on house current, and electricity in rural India is either unavailable or unreliable. So even if you could take the machine to a village, residents there would not have the means to operate it. Finally, the high-tech instrument can only be operated by a trained physician, but there are no such trained experts in rural India.

There was an obvious need for ECGs; rural Indians have the same health problems that other people do. However, this rural population couldn't consume the *business model* being offered to current consumers. GE's challenge, then, was to create a breakthrough—a Box 3 innovation—that could convert these nonconsumers to consumers.

In 2008, GE developed a $500 ECG machine, with which a single scan costs ten cents. Besides being affordable, this less expensive instrument is extraordinarily lightweight, weighing less than a can of Coke. It can be put in a backpack and taken door-to-door. And it is battery operated, producing 750 scans on a single charge. Furthermore, this innovative machine is extremely simple to operate. It has just two buttons: start and stop.

# PROCESS

The generation of Box 3 ideas has two parts—ideation and selection. How well you generate your ideas influences the success you'll have in selecting the single right one. Let's look at the two processes one by one.

## Creating an Environment Conducive to Ideas

To generate Box 3 ideas, you will need to organize an ideation session. A productive session requires preparation. In addition to making sure that the preliminary work of gathering the weak signals has been done, you'll want to assemble the right attendees in a comfortable environment, help them get in the right frame of mind, and facilitate the session so that they can build on each other's ideas, refine and synthesize those ideas, and report the ideas out.

### Attendees

You need to invite out-of-the-box thinkers to this session. In addition, invite people who have a passion for the subject or feel some ownership of the project.

When GE Healthcare conducted its Box 3 ideation, the members of the team were chosen carefully. The leaders selected twenty executives from inside the company, though not necessarily from the top. Each of the team members was a "maverick thinker" and relatively young, and most had worked for GE Healthcare for less than five years. GE Healthcare also chose twenty outsiders—hospital administrators, nonconsumers, health-care academics, government officials, and regulators to be on the team.

The forty-member team brainstormed Box 3 ideas for "good enough" medical imaging devices to be produced at an ultralow cost. Two things distinguished the team's output. First, the team could easily identify and understand a wide variety of weak signals and nonlinear shifts. Second, it had little vested interest in GE Healthcare's high-end medical imaging equipment.

## Setup

Team members need a comfortable place to be in a creative mind-set. Choose a location with fewer disturbances, an environment that is different from what people are used to. For instance, instead of conducting the exercise in an office conference room, find a place off-site. If, perhaps because of limited options, you do use an on-site conference room, change the room's decor. You might even put up posters or themed decorations to help people break out of their normal mental routines.

Ideally, have pop-up boards or whiteboards for each team so the participants can huddle around, discuss, and capture the ideas. Make sure to provide the necessary accessories, such as markers, sticky notes, tape, or sketching paper, at the outset.

Each team should have an assigned leader who is competent in facilitating the ideation session. When possible, it is always good to prearrange people in teams so that there is a good mix of individuals who offer a diversity of thought. You may even go to the extent of having name tags and designated seating in the room. This way, as soon as the attendees enter, they start getting comfortable with their teams. A round table is especially useful for facilitating equitable discussion.

Allocate enough time for the session so the teams don't feel rushed. At a minimum, spend half a day, preferably more, with the exercise.

## Warm-Up

To help the ideation attendees feel comfortable with each other, you may want to host a happy hour or dinner the previous night. If the attendees haven't been introduced before the session, start with an introduction coupled with an icebreaker exercise, such as a game, to help put the team members at ease with one another. One example of a game is Two Truths and a Lie. Each player makes three personal statements, two that are factual and one that isn't. The remaining team members have to guess which statement is not true. The goal should be to make team members aware of each other's background and expertise before the actual ideation exercise.

Give the teams a few minutes to formulate the ground rules for the ideation session. The members might, for example, agree that laptops stay closed unless someone is taking notes and that punctual returns from breaks are important, and they will set guidelines on whatever else they agree will help them work effectively.

Next, get the participants' creative juices flowing through a warm-up exercise, such as analogical thinking. For example, take two seemingly different things, perhaps one manufactured (e.g., a computer) and one from nature (e.g., a mountain). Ask each team member to jot down "How is a computer [first word] similar to a mountain [second word]?" We have often found that after people have written down their answers and subsequently discussed them, their initial ideas were simplistic but those at the end of the list are usually quite creative. Hence, be patient as you try to generate fifteen or more bullet points in your answer.

How is _____ similar to _____ ?

Once each person is familiar with the exercise, assign a new set of words and have them work in their assigned teams to answer the same question:

How is _____ similar to _____ ?

# HOW IS BATMAN SIMILAR TO A CHEF?

As children, we are very good at analogical thinking; we learn rapidly through association. But as we grow up, our creativity drops off.[1] In 1968, innovator and transformative thinker George Land gave eight tests of creative thinking to sixteen hundred children, three to five years old, who were enrolled in a Head Start program.[2] He found that 98 percent of them scored in the creative genius category. When the same children took identical tests five years later, roughly one-third scored that high. Five years after that, the proportion was down to 10 percent. Two hundred thousand adults over the age of twenty-five have taken the same tests and only 2 percent scored at the creative genius level. In *Breakpoint and Beyond: Mastering the Future Today*, Land and coauthor Beth Jarman say that the "socialization process restricts the natural creativity of our thinking potential by automatically assigning value judgments . . . [O]ur proficiency in expressing our creativity gradually drops off as we learn to accept others' opinions, evaluations, and beliefs."[3]

Here is an example of how Isha, a nine-year-old we recently spoke with, answered the question "How is Batman similar to a chef?"[4]

1. Both are human.

2. Both use technology. Batman uses technology to reach the crime scene quickly, and a chef uses technology, such as a blender, to cook effectively.

3. Both use tools. Batman has a "batarang," a bat-shaped boomerang, and a chef cooks using a chopping board.

4. Both wear something on their heads—Batman a masked hood, the chef a toque blanche (white hat).

5. Both handle weapons—Batman with guns, a chef with knives.

6. Both have assistants. Batman has Robin and his butler, Alfred, and a chef usually has an assistant chef.

7. Both are inventors. For instance, Batman invented his lie-detector machine, and a chef invents new recipes.

8. They both beat things. Batman beats villains. A chef beats eggs!

9. Both have come in contact with pies. Batman is attacked with crackling cream pies, the Joker's weapon containing crackling electricity. A chef makes pies for dessert.

10. Both use smoke. Batman uses smoke pellets, and a chef uses smoke to cook smoked turkey.

11. Both have uniforms that are *mostly* the same color throughout. Batman's uniform is black, while a chef's uniform is white.

12. Both have many fans. Top chefs have a fan following, as does Batman.

13. Both are on TV shows—for instance, *Batman: The Animated Series*. Chefs have cooking shows, such as *Iron Chef*.

14. Both have books written about them.

15. Both make things better. Batman makes Gotham City a safer place. Chefs make food in restaurants a delicious treat.

Try coming up with five more examples to get a feel for this exercise. It is precisely this sort of freewheeling thinking that helps get our creative juices flowing. With enough practice, you'll start to develop the skills needed to take ideas from one domain and apply them to another.

## Generating Ideas

Now, it's time to get down to business. First, present to all the teams the preliminary work on the weak signals that convey possible imagined futures for your industry. Allow the participants to digest the material and ask questions as needed. The purpose of the preliminary work is not only to provide food for thought, but also to form some boundaries for ideation to drive the discussion toward a Box 3 outcome consistent with your company's strategic intent.

Next, break into smaller teams, assign a team leader to each, and ask these teams to generate as many Box 3 ideas as possible. The desired outcome is to nurture divergent thinking, so operate under the rule "Every idea is a good idea" and build on ideas whenever possible. In this brainstorming session, no one should judge the ideas or try to select them. The team members do that separately after the ideas have been listed. Being nonjudgmental at this stage is critical to encourage the flow of ideas.

| Idea | Notes |
|------|-------|
| 1. | |
| 2. | |

| Idea | Notes |
|------|-------|
| 3. | |
| 4. | |
| 5. | |
| 6. | |
| 7. | |

*(continued)*

| Idea | Notes |
|---|---|
| 8. | |
| 9. | |
| 10. | |

The team leader's job is to capture the ideas as they are generated. A good facilitator will know when to move to the next idea and when to allow a discussion to trigger other ideas on which to build. The leader should keep tabs on people, encouraging those who are quiet or introverts to participate, to ensure that everyone has input. If one person or a few people are dominating the discussion, draw others in by asking for their ideas. People often become passionate about their ideas, and the leader can help move the discussion forward, attributing to each idea a fair value. At times it is also wise to remind the team to reflect back on the weak signals, particularly if idea generation stalls or diverges to something out of scope. You can encourage the participants to think of combining various weak signals or trends to see a different picture.

To stimulate ideas throughout the session, you might also assign roles, such as that of a competitor, an ecosystem partner, a consumer, or an enterprise.

## Honing Your Ideas

Once your team has generated ideas, you should use the last 15 to 25 percent of the team's time to refine the ideas so that they can be meaningfully articulated for selection of top ideas. Ensure that all the ideas are captured on digital or paper notes, recordings, and pictures so that you can refer to the ideas later if you need to.

_____

_____

_____

_____

_____

_____

_____

_____

_____

_____

## Selecting Ideas

Once you have generated a list of Box 3 ideas, you and your team will want to narrow your list. Doing so will take two steps.

**Step 1:** Evaluate the ideas based on your strategic intent, and categorize them as low, medium, or high.

| Idea | Fit with strategic intent (high, medium, or low) |
|------|--------------------------------------------------|
| 1. | |
| 2. | |
| 3. | |
| 4. | |
| 5. | |

| Idea | Fit with strategic intent (high, medium, or low) |
|---|---|
| 6. | |
| 7. | |
| 8. | |
| 9. | |
| 10. | |

**Step 2:** Discard the low-strategic-intent ideas. For the rest, evaluate each idea on attractiveness (low, medium, or high) and feasibility (low, medium, or high).

**Attractiveness of the idea:** What is the estimated total market size? What is the future growth potential?

**Feasibility, or fit with core competencies:** What is your ability to capture the market? How contested is the space? Are several competitors focused on a similar idea?

| Idea | Attractiveness | Feasibility |
|------|----------------|-------------|
| 1. | | |
| 2. | | |
| 3. | | |

| Idea | Attractiveness | Feasibility |
|------|----------------|-------------|
| 4. | | |
| 5. | | |
| 6. | | |
| 7. | | |
| 8. | | |

*(continued)*

| Idea | Attractiveness | Feasibility |
|------|----------------|-------------|
| 9.   |                |             |
| 10.  |                |             |

Next, have the smaller teams present to the entire group, their top ideas as well as their attractiveness and feasibility mapping and obtain the group's feedback. Ultimately, you want to pick ideas that are medium or high in each of the categories. If you encounter a trade-off between attractiveness and feasibility, always pick a *highly attractive market*, as you may be able to build, buy, or partner to fill capability gaps as long as you have some runway in capturing the market. If there is a tie between two or more highly attractive and feasible ideas, the entire group can vote to then select the top idea to incubate first.

## IDEAS IN PRACTICE

Imagine the year is 1995, when email use is beginning to ramp up. Hotmail, Yahoo!, and Google don't yet exist, internet connections are primarily through dial-up narrowband technology, and the leadership team at the New York Times Company is brainstorming Box 3 ideas. Some potential examples of the output are shown in the following table. Note that item 13 is grayed out, as it is not a true Box 3 idea. The proposal for NYTimes Autos, a new section dedicated to automobiles and included in the print newspaper, is an idea that relies on the present business model and hence is not a Box 3.

| Idea | Notes |
|---|---|
| 1. New York Times Digital (NYTD): an internet-based news provider | Could dramatically change the customer, the value proposition, and the value chain |
| 2. Extend *New York Times* newspaper to the Mexico market | Could target new customers with similar value, using the same value chain |
| 3. NYTimes Homes: a website for buying homes over the internet, eliminating the paper-based process | Could offer current and new *New York Times* customers the ability to buy a home online; new value for new customers that would require a new value chain, such as partnership with Fannie Mae or Freddie Mac |
| 4. NYTimes Creatives: internet-based ad making for third parties | Could provide internet-based, storytelling, or other advertising for advertisers to rebrand as their own |
| 5. À la carte offering: videos based on popular past *New York Times* articles distributed online and on TV | Could be targeted as a totally new service for nonconsumers |
| 6. NYTimes ISP: internet service provider | Could compete with AOL to provide internet dial-up narrowband service for consumers |
| 7. *NYTimes Lifestyle*: an online magazine | Online content that is different from, and could complement, *New York Times* printed content; a place where consumers could find more information after reading the printed newspaper |
| 8. NYTimes Newsgroup: an online discussion community | A moderated internet newsgroup for only *New York Times* customers to discuss and chat; added value for current newspaper customers |
| 9. NYTimes Books: publisher and seller of general books, textbooks, and medical journals | Could leverage the publishing capability to expand into books and journals |
| 10. NYTimes Radio: buying or partnering with radio stations all over the country | A different way to distribute the journalistic content |

*(continued)*

| Idea | Notes |
|------|-------|
| 11. NYTimes Tax: a tax-filing software to compete with Intuit | Building on the "trustworthy" *New York Times* brand and subscription base, could get into the software business distributing application CDs |
| 12. NYTimes Website Services: a services business that creates websites for other companies | Would require new customers, new value, and new value chain |
| 13. NYTimes Autos: a new section dedicated to autos in the print newspaper | A Box 1 idea; not a Box 3 idea |

Now, how would the NYTimes have culled this list? Recall its strategic intent we outlined in chapter 3: Whatever the weather, whatever the platform, the NYTimes will deliver the story that illuminates consumers' minds throughout the world and throughout their lives. Let's measure the ideas against that intent:

| Idea | Fit with strategic intent (high, medium, or low) | Rationale |
|------|--------------------------------------------------|-----------|
| 1. New York Times Digital (NYTD): an internet-based news provider | High | Stories on a new platform |
| 2. Extend *New York Times* newspaper to the Mexico market | High | A step in moving worldwide |
| 3. NYTimes Homes: a website for buying homes over the internet, eliminating the paper-based process | Low | Not about stories or journalism per se |
| 4. NYTimes Creatives: internet-based ad making for third parties | Medium | Leverages storytelling for ad making |
| 5. À la carte offering: videos based on popular past *New York Times* articles distributed online and on TV | High | New way of delivering stories; a new platform |
| 6. NYTimes ISP: internet service provider | Low | An attractive opportunity but not about stories or journalism |
| 7. *NYTimes Lifestyle*: an online magazine | High | Similar to a news website but with a narrow focus on a market segment |

| Idea | Fit with strategic intent (high, medium, or low) | Rationale |
|---|---|---|
| 8. NYTimes Newsgroup: an online discussion community | Medium | Complementary to the printed newspaper; helps "illuminate" the consumer mind |
| 9. NYTimes Books: publisher and seller of general books, textbooks, and medical journals | Low | Less about journalism and storytelling |
| 10. NYTimes Radio: buying or partnering with radio stations all over the country | Medium | Fits the universal platform-applicability direction identified in one of the strategic intent statements, but is a broader platform than just stories (e.g., music) |
| 11. NYTimes Tax: a tax-filing software to compete with Intuit | Low | Great market opportunity but not where the company wants to go |
| 12. NYTimes Website Services: a services business that creates websites for other companies | Low | Great opportunity as an early mover in internet technology (weak signal) but not the company's desired direction for its strategic intent |
| 13. NYTimes Autos: a new section dedicated to autos in the print newspaper | – | – |

Having discarded five (i.e., those that scored low) of the twelve ideas, we are now left with seven ideas we can evaluate against attractiveness and feasibility:

| Idea | Attractiveness | Feasibility |
|---|---|---|
| 1. New York Times Digital (NYTD): an internet-based news provider | High | Medium |
| 2. Extend *New York Times* newspaper to the Mexico market | Medium | High |
| 3. NYTimes Homes: a website for buying homes over the internet, eliminating the paper-based process | – | – |

*(continued)*

| Idea | Attractiveness | Feasibility |
| --- | --- | --- |
| 4. NYTimes Creatives: internet-based ad making for third parties | Medium | Low |
| 5. À la carte offering: videos based on popular past *New York Times* articles distributed online and on TV | Medium | Low |
| 6. NYTimes ISP: internet service provider | – | – |
| 7. *NYTimes Lifestyle*: an online magazine | Low | High |
| 8. NYTimes Newsgroup: an online discussion community | Medium | Medium |
| 9. NYTimes Books: publisher and seller of general books, textbooks, and medical journals | – | – |
| 10. NYTimes Radio: buying or partnering with radio stations all over the country | Medium | Low |
| 11. NYTimes Tax: tax-filing software to compete with Intuit | – | – |
| 12. NYTimes Website Services: a services business that makes websites for other companies | – | – |
| 13. NYTimes Autos: a new section dedicated to autos in the print newspaper | – | – |

Since we want to pick ideas that are either medium or high in both categories, we are left with the following ideas in priority order. Between items 1 and 2, we picked the idea with the more attractive market:

| Idea | Attractiveness | Feasibility |
| --- | --- | --- |
| 1. New York Times Digital (NYTD): an internet-based news provider | High | Medium |
| 2. Extend *New York Times* newspaper to the Mexico market | Medium | High |

| Idea | Attractiveness | Feasibility |
|---|---|---|
| 3. NYTimes Homes: a website for buying homes over the internet, eliminating the paper-based process | – | – |
| 4. NYTimes Creatives: internet-based ad making for third parties | – | – |
| 5. À la carte offering: videos based on popular past *New York Times* articles distributed online and on TV | – | – |
| 6. NYTimes ISP: internet service provider | – | – |
| 7. *NYTimes Lifestyle*: an online magazine | – | – |
| 8. NYTimes Newsgroup: an online discussion community | Medium | Medium |
| 9. NYTimes Books: publisher and seller of general books, textbooks, and medical journals | – | – |
| 10. NYTimes Radio: buying or partnering with radio stations all over the country | – | – |
| 11. NYTimes Tax: a tax-filing software to compete with Intuit | – | – |
| 12. NYTimes Website Services: a services business that creates websites for other companies | – | – |
| 13. NYTimes Autos: a new section dedicated to autos in the print newspaper | – | – |

# Wrap-Up

The fourth step in ideation—brainstorming and identifying as many Box 3 ideas as possible—pulls together the understanding you've gained from examining your business and forecasting the market environment. Your Box 3 ideas should exploit the unique place your organization might fit in the future. We've made several observations about how to create these Box 3 ideas:

- Market discontinuities, strategic intent, and core competencies set the context for brainstorming.

- Box 3 ideas typically lie at the intersection of two or more market discontinuities.

- Box 3 ideas must be rank-ordered according to the market size of the opportunity, the company's ability to capture the opportunity, and the idea's fit with strategic intent.

- Rigorously debate the ideas to finally pick the topmost idea for incubation.

PART
TWO

# INCUBATION

In this part of the book, we outline how you move from an idea to a go/no-go decision. A comfortable *go* decision, for example, would be signing up the first paying customer in a B2B context. Getting to a go/no-go decision involves further developing the idea into a pitch, gaining internal sponsors, and securing initial resources to validate some key assumptions (most of them customer-centric at this stage). You need to complete the steps of this incubation stage before moving on to a formal initiative with a long-term commitment from management—the scale phase, which is covered in part 3.

# 6

# TESTING CRITICAL ASSUMPTIONS

As we kick off the incubation stage, keep in mind three important points. First, what you have right now is a Box 3 idea with a zero-dollar value. At this stage, your Box 3 idea is simply a thought experiment. Since no value has been created, it is worth *zero* dollars. In fact, considering the labor cost of your team to brainstorm the idea, the value may even be negative. You will travel the road ahead one step at a time to create value as you demonstrate that your idea's value proposition is desirable, feasible, and monetizable. The day you land your first paying customer is truly when the value creation speeds up and when the idea is worth something meaningful. Strive to reach this milestone quickly and cheaply.

Second, your idea is just a set of assumptions. For example, as the NYTimes pursued NYTD, its digital Box 3 idea, the company didn't know whether the internet would take off, what the rate of broadband penetration would be, or whether the *New York Times* brand equity would translate to a different medium and a different audience. These were just a set of assumptions. Thus, your primary task in the incubation period is to test your assumptions and convert them into knowledge. Strive to reduce the assumptions-to-knowledge ratio.

Finally, focus on the critical assumptions and unknowns. Critical assumptions are those that if proven false have fatal consequences for the project. Either it is game over for the project or the project requires a significant pivot. In our experience, critical assumptions in the incubation stage largely center around the customer. You must validate an unmet need and the customers' willingness to pay.

Once you are reasonably confident that the critical assumptions hold true, you can move to the next stage in the innovation process. While scaling a Box 3 experiment, you need to test a residual set of assumptions. We will discuss this in further detail in part 3.

Given that the idea at the start of the incubation process is a set of assumptions, your goal is to test the most critical assumptions and convert them into knowledge. You need to do this, however, without spending a lot of money. This is what we mean by "low-cost experiments." Let's look at three types of assumptions you need to examine during the incubation stage of your Box 3 ideas.[1]

## Customer-Centric and Market-Centric Assumptions

Will the customer want your solution? Customer-centric assumptions are the most important to test in the incubation phase. Moreover, you need to remember that customers' expectations are always rising. The cool features of today become the basic or must-have features of tomorrow.

Thomas Edison, one of the world's most prolific inventors of all time, learned his lesson on being customer-focused the hard way.[2] Edison had invented and patented a vote-counting machine that he attempted to sell to lawmakers. His invention would have enabled lawmakers not only to cast votes from their seats, but also to have an accurate count available immediately. At that time, however, legislators preferred a delay in casting and counting so that they could lobby for their side and change the results. Disappointed that there was no market for his valuable invention, Edison promised himself not to waste time inventing things people didn't want to buy.

In 2012, Jibo, Inc., founded by high-profile robotics experts, was building the first-ever social robot for the home. Jibo's announcement made headlines in 2014, when smart assistants and chat bots were the next big thing. However, unlike robots that have proven quite useful in countries like Japan to improve the lives of elderly people, Jibo lacked a clear value proposition. When the device launched, reviewers found that the product offered "limited utility" in a world where Alexa (Amazon), Google Assistant, and Siri (Apple) provided many capabilities without the $900 price tag of a Jibo robot.[3] In March 2019, Jibo the social robot, which had even made *Time* magazine's best inventions list in 2017, had shut down its servers and was bidding farewell to its users.[4]

## Development-Centric Assumptions

Can you build the solution you plan to offer? This question represents the crux of development. In the 1990s, for example, IBM decided to develop a supercomputer, Blue Gene, that was one thousand times faster than the fastest computer then in existence. It was designed for geneticists who needed extremely high-performance computing to conduct their studies. The customer, as well as the market, was clearly evident. If IBM could build such a product, the company could sell it. But despite the tremendous advances in processor sophistication and speed, faster processors also consumed a lot of power. This meant that traditional approaches to building Blue Gene wouldn't work. Thus, IBM made a key assumption that it could find an alternative paradigm to build Blue Gene.

## Monetization-Centric Assumptions

Will you be able to make money? Let's look at how two companies examined this question. Since IBM's Blue Gene was aimed at the highest end of the performance computing market, where there was a clear, unmet demand for a product that didn't yet exist, the ability to recover Blue Gene's costs may have been less of an issue for the company. The case of Webvan, however, presents a different story. During the dot-com boom in the 1990s, Webvan sought to be an online grocery business. Its value proposition was to offer greater convenience than what traditional grocery stores offered—for example, a thirty-minute free-delivery window. It also advertised lower product prices than found at traditional stores. Webvan took its first orders in 1999 but burned through over $1 billion in cash and shut down in 2001. The company's assumption about its sales-to-expenses ratio proved false. Another key assumption was the average order size (in dollars) that was required to sustain the company in 2000 and 2001. The company missed that number by more than 20 percent in those years.[5]

---

When Blue Gene was conceived, the IBM team members assumed they could assemble a supercomputer using commodity processors, as opposed to fast processors, to overcome the power-consumption issue. However, the theoretical limit on the number of chips that could be used in the configuration was 512, a number based on a research paper. They conducted low-cost experiments by incrementally doubling the number of chips from their previous iterations to test their assumption. Their experiments led the team to build a supercomputer with more than 8,000 chips.

IBM's experience leads us to an incubation mantra: "Try it and see if it works . . . without harming Box 1." Every innovation initiative is uncertain; failure *is* an option when the critical assumptions don't pan out. In fact, the chance of failure is quite high. Therefore, running the incubation initiative under the radar, avoiding unnecessary internal and external marketing, may be fine at this stage. It may also help avoid the "shiny" new object perception. In other words, don't count your chickens until they are hatched.

# PROCESS

Incubation is the journey to take an idea from conception to a go/no-go decision. The journey involves the following steps:

1. Identify a sponsor or champion.

2. Create an idea pitch.

3. Sell the pitch to obtain a sponsor or champion, funds, and some resources to test your critical assumptions—assumptions that if proven false are fatal to the success of the project.

4. Test these critical assumptions through low-cost experiments that culminate in a go/no-go decision.

## Identifying a Sponsor or Champion

In established companies, incubation initiatives need to be protected and nurtured, or there is little chance they will survive. The most important step is finding a sponsor or champion who will take the responsibility to support the effort. This champion must be a seasoned executive with credibility across your organization. It may very well be the CEO. In addition to protecting and funding the incubation initiative, the champion has the important role of opening doors to potential customers and the needed resources. When budgets are tight or Box 1 is in danger of potential damage from Box 3 initiatives, the sponsor can also play a critical role in communicating the vision of the incubation initiative. This person can tell a better story of how Box 3 can operate in harmony with Box 1.

Typically, you may have two choices for where to host the incubation initiative: either inside a Box 1 or in a separate organization that is tasked with creating and evaluating new business ventures. Hosting the incubation in Box 1 has a few advantages. It is easier to borrow resources if they are needed, and you can bring your organization on board throughout the journey to a go/no-go decision, obtaining buy-in in the process. The trick, however, is to ensure that the initiative is not buried in your organization and constrained by the operational tempo of Box 1. One way to solve this issue is to have the incubation initiative report up to the sponsor.

By contrast, the advantage of incubating the initiative in a dedicated organization tasked with running many such projects is that you can build competencies in incubations and can leverage the learning from one initiative to another. The disadvantage is that you have to amplify your selling or adoption efforts to a business unit if the initiative will ultimately reside there at scale-up.

Think of the potential sponsors or champion candidates who meet the following criteria, and write them on a list:

- Credibility within the organization

- A strong internal and external network

- Familiarity with the innovation journey (nonroutine, unpredictable, high rate of failure)

- Value to offer to the initiative (e.g., domain or market expertise) or value to gain from the initiative (e.g., complementary intellectual property [IP])

- The ability to keep you accountable to fail fast and cheap, learn, adjust, and continue with the work

- Good coaching and communication skills

## Creating an Idea Pitch

To create an idea pitch, you'll want to assemble a virtual team comprising people who have a passion for the idea, domain expertise, and the bandwidth or time. Given that your Box 3 idea is still just a concept, the team has to spend time making the idea sellable as well as executable. *Sellable* implies that busy executives who were not a part of the Box 3 brainstorming can nevertheless quickly comprehend the idea. *Executable* means that enough next steps are planned out so that once an idea is given the green light, even someone uninvolved in it can pick it up and hit the ground running. Let's sketch what you need to do for your idea pitch.

## FINDING A CHAMPION AT PROCTER & GAMBLE

In the mid-1990s, P&G embarked on a new initiative to explore whether out-licensing IP assets that were lying unused on the shelf within P&G could generate a new revenue stream.[6] P&G created a small pilot incubation team, Global Licensing, consisting of about a dozen people, to test the hypothesis.

Even though an experienced vice president/general manager was assigned to lead the project, the team ran into obstacles, particularly because the project was established as a profit center. First, no group was incentivized to provide the team with IP assets, because the benefit or revenue would accrue to the Global Licensing group, not to the business unit providing the unused IP. Second, since the group was an experiment, it had no visible endorsement from the leadership team.

Global Licensing's first milestone—generating more revenue than the team's overhead costs—would not have been possible had it not been for the support of the group vice president for P&G's snacks and beverage business. This executive was a strong supporter of the project. The head of the snacks division's R&D pointed to a patented technology, calcium citrate malate, or CCM, as a potential licensing candidate.

Although CCM was an innovative technology with tremendous potential, it was a leftover from businesses that had unsuccessfully attempted to sell orange juice products and had subsequently shut down. With strong patent protection, clinical results, formulation expertise, market differentiation, and ease of integration into other formulations or products, CCM proved to be a good asset to bet on.

Ultimately, Global Licensing formed a partnership with Tropicana, which successfully commercialized CCM. With the initiative generating its first revenue, other internal groups saw the value of the initiative, and support resources started flowing to the team. The champion's willingness to believe in the project and take smart risks was one of the most critical factors in ensuring the team's survival.

## Write Your Elevator Pitch

Describe your idea in three to five words on the lines below. Such a description, which concisely communicates an idea to a senior executive and is built on what the executive already knows, is a great tool to grab attention and differentiate it from other requests the executive may be facing. You should be able to describe your idea in about twenty seconds.

_____

_____

_____

_____

In the 1960s, *New York Times* food editor Craig Claiborne gathered numerous *Times* recipes and created his own cookbook, which turned out to be a hit. In early 2017, the NYTimes launched a Box 3 idea: a dedicated, separate-subscription website that targeted foodies with curated cooking content. In an era when recipes are a commodity and easily available on the internet, this idea would be an interesting challenge.

## NETFLIX FOR GAMES

In January 2019, Microsoft was pursuing a Box 3 idea for a streaming service for games. Playing games currently requires purchase of a device, such as an Xbox, that connects to a TV. Microsoft's Box 3 idea is to create a service that allows gamers to stream their games of choice on any device—phone, tablet, laptop, or TV—without requiring an expensive, power-hungry console. It would be a service similar to Netflix. In fact, Microsoft internally calls the service "Netflix for games."

*Source:* Ben Gilbert, "Microsoft Is Creating the 'Netflix for Games': Here's Everything We Know So Far," *Business Insider*, March 13, 2019, www.businessinsider.com/microsoft-xbox-netflix-for-games-2019-1.

Given the past success of Claiborne's *New York Times Cook Book*, however, describing the website as a digital version of the best seller is a much better opening pitch statement than calling the venture yet another cooking website.

## Identify the Opportunities

Answer these questions about opportunity. Presenting this part of the pitch to a sponsor can take up to five minutes.

1. Who is your target customer?

   _____

   _____

   _____

   _____

2. What is your perceived customer need or pain point, and why do you believe that this need exists? (For instance, does the pain point have a precedent? Does it come from another domain? From actual customer feedback?)

   _____

   _____

   _____

   _____

3. What is your proposed solution?

   _____

   _____

   _____

   _____

4. How does it solve the customer's pain point?

_____

_____

_____

_____

5. Why should this Box 3 idea be pursued *now*?

_____

_____

_____

_____

6. What is the high-level total addressable market (TAM) for the opportunity?

_____

_____

_____

_____

Imagine you are the founder of Airbnb, where members can use the service to book or offer lodging. Furthermore, suppose you believe that people will rent rooms in strangers' homes. Now imagine that a person listening to the pitch reacts badly to the idea of living in strangers' homes. You could overcome this objection by pointing out that this practice was, in fact, normal in the past.[7] The bed-and-breakfast concept has been around for centuries all over the world. For instance, monasteries offered lodging to travelers. In the United States during the Great Depression, people used their homes as boardinghouses to generate revenue.

In the NYTimes cooking website example above, the fact that a cookbook had been a best seller was one belief underlying the perceived customer need. Of course, the previous success didn't mean the company could just repurpose old microwave recipes and hope for a home run. It did have to figure out a value proposition that resonated with today's foodies. This meant revamping some evergreen recipes from the 1960s and 1970s by rephotographing the dishes to create high-resolution images and augmenting the photos with videos to cater to today's consumer taste.

## Explain How You Can Beat the Competition

Next, you tell the potential sponsor how you can beat the competition. This part of the pitch can take up to five minutes.

Executives listening to your presentation may focus on two things at this point. First, is this a large TAM opportunity? Second, is this a market the company should enter? You've already addressed the question of TAM opportunity in the questions you answered in the preceding "Identify the Opportunities" section.

In addition, articulate why you believe your organization can reach a leadership position. It is important to assess your competition. What if entering the market puts you in competition with your customers or with entrenched giants against which it may be hard to compete?

Imagine, for instance, that you are the executive pitching Amazon's entry into the brick-and-mortar grocery business. Showing that it is a large TAM opportunity is easy. The key challenge is articulating how you'll use Amazon's core strengths of customer intimacy, data-driven decision making, Amazon Prime services, and customer base to win against Walmart, the nine-hundred-pound gorilla. Write down your answers to the following questions to be better prepared for your sponsor's questions:

1. Why do you believe the TAM is high? (Use your work from the previous exercise.)

_____

_____

_____

_____

_____

_____

2. Who are your key competitors? Executives in your organization will want to know whether you plan to enter a crowded market with big players or a market with just a few key players.

_____

_____

_____

_____

_____

_____

3. Why us? Why will we win? What is our differentiation and sustainable advantage?

_____

_____

_____

_____

_____

_____

For NYT Cooking, the team believed its database of recipes from over the years and its knowledge of those that were successful and etched into consumers' minds was the differentiation that would allow it to win customers.

## Highlight Three to Five Critical Assumptions

As described at the beginning of the chapter, if critical assumptions are proven false, they can doom the project. This part of the pitch—explaining your critical assumptions—should take up to ten minutes and should be specific. For example, a critical assumption of the NYT Cooking team might be, "A meaningful number of cooking enthusiasts will be willing to pay an extra $5 a month for access to a *New York Times* cooking service." Answer the following questions pertaining to the three types of assumptions you make in developing your Box 3 idea:

- **Customer-centric:** Will customers want it?

  _____

  _____

  _____

  _____

  _____

  _____


- **Development-centric:** Can we build it?

  _____

  _____

  _____

  _____

_____

_____

- **Monetization-centric:**  Can we make money?

_____

_____

_____

_____

_____

_____

## Prove How You'll Test Critical Assumptions

In the incubation stage, the golden rule is "Spend a little, learn a lot." You should be able to articulate how, while incurring little cost, you'll test assumptions—and fail fast if they are invalid.

To test the aforementioned critical assumption that a meaningful number of cooking enthusiasts will be willing to pay an extra $5 for access to the _New York Times_ cooking website, the NYTimes could have tried some low-cost experiments.

It could have visited places where cooking enthusiasts are likely to hang out, such as cooking classes at Sur La Table and other popular kitchen supply stores or a culinary school in a zip code with high _New York Times_ readership. The NYTimes could distribute to these potential customers a marketing brochure or video offering a trial rate of $5 per month. The offer could include a full money-back guarantee (if the service failed to meet the consumer's needs or be delivered on time) within a certain period. If a meaningful number of people were to pay the deposit, the NYTimes could have validated the assumption through these revealed preferences. Another option would have been to run an online campaign, like Kickstarter. The experiment may not be needed at all if the company looked externally and found a magazine already offering a similar service to paying customers.

Brainstorm some ways your organization could test your critical assumptions quickly and at a low cost.

---------------------------------------------------------------

---------------------------------------------------------------

---------------------------------------------------------------

---------------------------------------------------------------

---------------------------------------------------------------

## Selling Your Idea

Now you must sell the pitch to obtain a sponsor or champion, the necessary funds, and other resources to test your critical assumptions. Brainstorm with your team to decide what resources you will need to complete the project. You should be able to justify why you need these. Let's now look at some of these necessary resources.

### Project Manager

Although some resources may very well be only temporarily required during incubation, the project manager must be a dedicated full-time resource. Pick a person with an entrepreneurial mind-set—someone able to get things done even without formal authority or direct control over other resources—and preferably with some market or domain expertise. This role could be a great development opportunity for a rising star who is not risk-averse and is excited about the potential opportunity.

The sponsor or leader must be accessible to the project manager to help navigate the project when needed. Thus, picking a person who is either familiar to the sponsor or able to report directly to the sponsor for the duration of the project is a good idea. The ideal project manager will be familiar with strategy, design, development, and marketing.

Sometimes, the domain expertise isn't available in the company. In that case, be open to hiring externally for this position.

In the following space, list the candidates for project manager:

_____

_____

_____

_____

## Budget

You and the team need to estimate the budget required for testing your critical assumptions and reaching a go/no-go conclusion. These funds must be earmarked for a certain period but will be spent *gradually* and will be continuously adjusted according to feedback from the low-cost experiments.

On the following lines, note your budget and time frame:

_____

_____

_____

_____

## Internal Resources

In the incubation phase, the project manager will require a small team made up of part-time and full-time staff who collectively bring together expertise in the domains of desirability, feasibility, and viability. For tasks that are similar to routine work in your organization, such as finance, borrowing part-time staff could suffice. For areas that require new thinking, dedicated staff work best.

In the NYT Cooking example, a dedicated resource could be someone who will sift through cooking recipes the *New York Times* has published over the years and decide which ones are ripe for revival. Additionally, the team could use a photographer from the *Times* to create new high-resolution images.

On the following lines, list the internal help your project needs:

_____

_____

_____

_____

## External Resources

To test critical assumptions for your project, you may need access to targeted customers, partners, skill sets, and technology. These must be listed so that the sponsor can help champion, connect, and accelerate progress.

What if these skills aren't available in your organization? One alternative to hiring and building a team from scratch is forming partnerships. Another is acquisitions.

When the electric car company Tesla was starting out, it used partnerships to complement missing capabilities in the company.[8] Building an entire car from scratch would have been too expensive in terms of human, as well as financial, capital. Thus, Tesla's approach was to build on an existing car. After evaluating several manufacturers of light-weight, midrange-engine cars, Tesla ended up partnering with Lotus Cars, a British automaker. The partnership eventually provided tremendous learning to Tesla, which had never built cars before. In fact, six months after meeting with Malcolm Powell, a project manager at Lotus, Tesla executives hired him as the vice president of vehicle integration. Another key missing skill for Tesla was design. While the company's engineers had a vision for the design, communicating that vision to designers was not easy. As a result, the first proposals for designs that Tesla received didn't hit the mark. Only when Tesla engaged IDEO cofounder Bill Moggridge, who was able to translate the vision into what designers understood, did the company find styling designs that matched its vision.

Write down the skill sets, technology, and other resources you may be lacking and hence may need to source externally.

_____

_____

_____

_____

## Metrics and Kill Switches

Testing a critical assumption can produce either of two useful outcomes: a positive result or a negative result. Negative results are not bad; they just mean you have to either pivot or kill the initiative. To monitor progress, you must define the metrics up front. You need to define what constitutes a positive result and a negative result and decide on the impact of a negative result—whether you will treat the negative result as a kill switch or a pivot trigger.

For the NYT Cooking example, one of the key metrics could be stated as follows: "Ten thousand _New York Times_ nonsubscribers and five hundred subscribers signed up for the online service in six months." A kill switch could be this result: "The cost structure of producing the service doesn't support the desired gross margins, inclusive of a 10 percent buffer."

On the lines below, define the metrics you will use and what results would force you to kill the project:

_____

_____

_____


### Timeline and Milestones

To make sure you keep your Box 3 idea on track, use the space below to note the milestones you expect to hit for your project and the approximate time these milestones will take.

_____

_____

_____


## Anticipating What to Do If the Answer Is No

In established organizations, executives hear pitches day in, day out in the midst of fighting urgent fires. Not many ideas see the light of day. People who generate ideas can sometimes feel as if they are fighting an uphill battle to get an approval. If your pitch is not making it through, reflect on the following possibilities.

**It's the idea.** One possibility is that the idea itself is not gaining traction for one or more of the following reasons:

- The idea hasn't been fleshed out well, and the pitch is weak.

- Even if you assume that you will be wildly successful in executing the idea, it fails when you ask, "Will it matter to the company?"

- The idea is not material enough to move the needle. Maybe even as a highly successful venture, the gross margins will be below corporate gross margins and have an adverse impact.

- Incubation requires taking key resources away from Box 1 and harms Box 1 in the near term. It is a distraction for the management team.

Getting objective feedback in a preliminary meeting from people you and your company respect is one way to get clarity on this topic before pitching the idea.

**It's the idea's timing.** At any given time, a company will have a portfolio of projects and ideas in the works. These Box 3 ideas will range from those that are adjacent to the core to those that are disruptive to the core. The company can only take on a limited number of bets. For example, maybe there is already an idea in the "disruptive" bucket; if so, management may be reluctant to fund more ideas like this. The further an idea is from the core, the higher is its execution risk. Perhaps your organization is not ready to take on additional incremental execution risk at this time. Assessing the environment and the way the wind is blowing is a perspective the potential sponsor can offer.

**It's you.** Another possibility is that you as an individual don't yet have a voice or credibility in the organization. Or worse, you have negative credibility, having cried wolf too many times previously. People often lack a voice or credibility when they are new to an organization and not specifically tasked with driving incubation initiatives. People have negative credibility when they have a track record of negative personal-brand equity. In this situation, executives are not even listening to good ideas because the person's (lack of) believability is standing in the way. One way to improve your odds is to partner with someone who has high credibility and do a joint presentation or, alternatively, have the other person pitch the idea.

**It's them. Sorry, but it's still you!** One typical reaction to a rejection is feeling that the audience doesn't get it. You may fall into the trap of saying that the audience is not imaginative or they can't see the trend or the executives lack an innovative mind-set. While these observations may very well be true, it is still *your* responsibility to help others visualize the idea and to persuade them. In these matters, persistence pays off. Listen to others' objections, go back, revamp, and pitch again. Perhaps create an abbreviated version of your video of the future to help them overcome their lack of imagination. An inspirational example is Corning Inc.'s "A Day Made of Glass" video from 2011.[11] The third time you pitch your ideas may be a charm. You may get another advocate in the company to join forces with you, perhaps by showing them what's in it for them. This is where your sales skills need to shine.

## Validating Assumptions Quickly and Cheaply

Now you need to test critical assumptions through low-cost experiments that will culminate in a go/no-go decision. Before you start building prototypes, you must test customer-centric assumptions first. In other words, if you build it, will they come?

Consider the example of IBM's speech-to-text experiment.[9] In the 1980s, IBM wanted to know whether customers would be interested in a system that automatically converted users' speech to text. Instead of spending a lot of money building a prototype—an expensive proposition in an era when computer processing power wasn't cheap—and tackling the formidable computer science problem of converting generalized speech to text, IBM conducted a low-cost experiment. The company invited people who were excited about this possibility to a room equipped with a microphone and computer terminal but no keyboard. The subjects were asked to speak into the microphone, and the words automatically appeared on screen. What the subjects didn't know at the time was that there was no technology in place; there was simply an individual in an adjacent room typing the subjects' speech. Without this knowledge, the subjects could experience the idea and react as if the system truly existed. IBM discovered that the subjects didn't respond favorably to the experience, for a variety of reasons. Thus, the company tested a critical assumption quickly and cheaply.

Testing assumptions is a great opportunity to challenge accepted beliefs and ask questions to uncover the truth. A great example is from Kevin Rose's interview of Elon Musk. The entrepreneur describes a "first principles" approach—questioning everything you know:

> Somebody could say . . . that battery packs are really expensive and that's just the way they will always be because that's the way they've been in the past . . . Historically, it has cost six hundred dollars per kilowatt-hour. It's not going to be much better than that in the future . . .
>
> With first principles, you say, "What are the material constituents of the batteries? What is the stock market value of the material constituents?" You can say, "Okay, it's got cobalt, nickel, aluminum, carbon, and some polymers for separation and a steel can." Break that down on a materi-al[s] basis and say, "If we bought that on the London Metal Exchange, what would each of those things cost?" It's like eighty per kilowatt-hour. So, clearly, you just need to think of clever ways to take those materials and combine them into the shape of a battery cell, and you can have batteries that are much, much cheaper than anyone realizes.[10]

Another way to resolve a critical unknown is to study whether anyone else has encountered and solved this problem. Is there academic research you can rely on? Have any startups demonstrated similar projects at conferences? What about your company's ecosystem partners and their innovation efforts?

On the lines below, jot down where else you might look to find evidence that can validate your assumptions.

_____

_____

_____

_____

Sometimes, companies that are missing key strategic competencies will acquire early-stage companies that may have made some progress testing some assumptions and gotten closer to a product-market fit. The acquisition may be motivated by the smaller company's technology and talent, regardless of the success of the specific Box 3 idea the startup may be pursuing at the time. Buying versus building can potentially accelerate the idea's time to market. In certain cases, the buy option may be able to skip the entire incubation process.

In the mid-2000s, for example, Adobe was known as a Photoshop company. Photoshop was a world-class product, but it was also pirated heavily. Adobe's business model was the traditional software licensing model at the time. Its product development launch cycles were roughly eighteen months long, during which time the company would add features, raise prices, and drive product refresh.

New CEO Shantanu Narayen and his leadership team saw the opportunity to transform the company into a content marketing company and change its business model to software as a service. This transformation was a tremendously difficult move to make as it changed how value was created and sold. A subscription model would price products much lower and require faster innovative updates in terms of product life cycles. However, not only did Adobe recognize the importance of data, but the company also saw signals that engaging consumers online was going to be extremely important. Furthermore, the leadership realized that no single company then owned that space.

One option for Adobe would have been to hire in a web-analytics team and build the competency from scratch. However, given the mammoth opportunity, the desire to build on its digital-creation competencies, and the need for rapid growth, Adobe acquired Omniture, a public web-analytics company, in 2009 to enter the market. The acquisition laid the foundation of growth for the company in the coming decade. Adobe successfully transformed its business model to a subscription business. In 2012, revenues from its Creative Cloud and Marketing Cloud (later renamed Experience Cloud) apps were in the hundreds of millions of dollars, and by 2016, they were more than $4 billion.

# IDEAS IN PRACTICE

Imagine it is the late 1990s and you are an executive at AirEng, a hypothetical firm that manufactures aircraft engines. AirEng sells engines to airlines for their planes, such as the Airbus A380. The firm's current business model is selling hardware (engines) to create an installed base of engines and making money on break-fix service contracts for the life of the engines; when the engines break, AirEng services them for a fee. While there is some software in the products, AirEng gives it away to drive adoption of its engines and increase its installed base. AirEng has lately had tremendous success. The company now powers twenty types of commercial aircraft, and the latest engine line, Engine 98, has been chosen by nine of the twelve operators. Let's examine how you could go through the process as outlined above.

## Reflecting on Weak Signals

Industrywide development of advanced high-thrust engines in the 1980s caused many of the hydromechanical engine-control systems to be replaced by full-authority digital electronics control systems to accommodate handling numerous engine parameters. Attributes such as fan speed, altitude, and temperature are now gathered through electronic control systems such as thermocouples and transducers. These advancements have increased engine durability and reliability.

As a result, spare-engine demand in the future is declining rapidly. In the golden days, AirEng's highly profitable and higher-priced spare engines used to equal the value of a regular-engine sale over five to ten years. Looking ahead, your team forecasts that a spare engine's value will be equal to the value of a regular engine over twenty-five years.

AirEng's Box 1 business was all about creating the widest product portfolio and spreading the R&D costs across multiple products. For instance, a lightweight titanium fan could be applied to various engine types. However, in the industry future that you imagine, you recognize the need to pursue a Box 3 idea to strategically extract more value from the installed base of engines, selling not just spare parts but maintenance services as well. Furthermore, these services must be offered *differently* from how current Box 1 service contracts are executed.

In Box 1, service contract incentives were misaligned. Customers were serviced when their planes were down, and AirEng had little control over support costs. Just last month, a key customer told you to expect a larger-than-expected number of engines coming in for servicing.

As you look around the ecosystem, you see a weak signal. A young startup company is offering your customers software for engine data analysis and the promise of predictive maintenance. If the startup is successful, it could further siphon off your revenues. You wonder, What if AirEng could guarantee increased fuel efficiency to customers, using its knowledge of engine data, and align the service contract incentives with customers so that they only paid for services when needed?

You realize such a Box 3 idea not only will receive pushback from management but also will require different skill sets (data scientists versus mechanical engineers) and competencies (customized contracts versus standard contracts) that are not present in the company today. Believing that the right sponsor for this initiative would be the CEO, you start creating your pitch to present at the next executive sync (or update) meeting. Using the process outlined above in the "Creating an Idea Pitch" section, you would break your pitch into several steps. Let's consider them now.

## Elevator Pitch

You plan to grab the attention of the CEO and other stakeholders by giving your Box 3 idea a short, understandable description. In this case, you've chosen "fixed price per flying hour" to get your idea across.

## Opportunity

You've already decided on each of these elements of your pitch:

- **Target customer:** Your target market is the same as today's market, as well as nonairline industrial companies.

- **Customer pain point:** Customers want to align payment with engines that are performing well. They want to reduce unscheduled downtime and increase fuel efficiency, both of which directly translate to their bottom line. You have learned of these desires through several customer conversations. In fact, a key customer is sending you a larger-than-expected engine-servicing request for which you have not budgeted.

- **Proposed solution:** You want to offer increased fuel efficiency to customers, using digital software tools. You can perform big-data and business intelligence analysis on engine parameters to derive insights that can be used to predict maintenance. You can guarantee increased fuel efficiency to help customers manage their operational costs better, and you can share the value you create in the process.

- **How the solution works:** The solution will align your incentives with customer outcomes. Every 1 percent increase in fuel efficiency translates to $1 billion in customers' bottom lines. The data analysis capabilities will reduce unscheduled downtime for customers and provide better control over your support costs. You can sell the solution not only to your current customers but also to nonairline industrial companies looking for such software tools.

- **Reasons to pursue the solution now:** There are multiple reasons for taking action now. Your spare-parts business, where profit margins are seven times those of engines, is suffering from declining demand going forward. Thus, you need new ideas to replenish the revenue. Industry signals are pointing in this direction as well. Airlines are cutting costs and looking to outsource maintenance operations. The customer sending a larger-than-expected engine-servicing request will probably be willing to explore this possibility with you.

## Competition

To present the key competitors, show the CEO and other potential sponsors a slide illustrating the value proposition of a company that is already offering predictive maintenance to customers today, but redact the company's name.

Ask the audience to guess which company this is. The participants will probably guess competing aircraft engine companies, but plan to surprise them by revealing the name of the software company. Show them the maintenance, repair, and overhaul market players that could be potential competitors. Given that the market is fragmented and currently focused only narrowly on maintenance, you believe that AirEng is well positioned to grab share from competitors and expand through the new proposed solution to enlarge the TAM for service revenues.

Explain that the question of why you will win can be answered by your company's core competency of knowledge about engines, which are highly sophisticated equipment. At the same time, emphasize this idea represents new space for AirEng and you will need new skills and capabilities to build a sustainable advantage.

## Critical Assumptions

One of AirEng's key critical assumptions is the following: Software can create significant incremental value over hardware sales, and the customer will be willing to share this increase in value with AirEng.

How might AirEng test this assumption with a low-cost experiment? You can see that the critical assumption has two key unknowns: Does the software provide meaningful incremental value for the customer? Is the customer willing to pay a part of that value to AirEng?

To answer these questions, AirEng must pick a potential target customer to engage with, and more importantly, it must prepare for a meaningful conversation with that customer. The desired outcome of this meeting would be a commitment from the customer in terms of a deposit or an advance payment—a clear success criterion.

For a deposit to be paid, the customer must be able to visualize the final product, even if it is not functional at this stage, and have some confidence that AirEng can deliver. One way you can meet that requirement is by analyzing the customer's currently available engine data over a period, leveraging AirEng's installed base of hardware, and demonstrating insights that can result in cost savings for the customer. Additionally, you can show that these savings are not a onetime occurrence but can be achieved repeatedly by automating the software in conjunction with AirEng's hardware road map.

Hence, your first meeting with the customer may be about sharing AirEng's hypothesis and getting buy-in to use the customer's data for the company's low-cost experiment. AirEng can use its prior relationship with the customer to get permission to access the customer's engine data.

## Assumptions Testing

Now the onus is on AirEng to demonstrate a few additional success criteria. The company needs to establish a clear relationship between the customer's flight performance data and AirEng's engines. If there is no relationship between these two elements, the customer might experience a garbage-in/garbage-out situation. For example, if the flight performance data is not accurately assessing the engine's condition or if there are dependencies that are not being comprehensively captured in the data, the accuracy of the output or insights will be questionable.

Next, the data you analyze must demonstrate that a meaningful number of engines require maintenance less frequently than others do. The data must also show that some maintenance could have been predicted at a more opportune time to avoid unscheduled downtime for the customer and to save the customer maintenance costs. Furthermore, you should quantify the savings in conjunction with a reduction in spare engine requirements for the customer. This analysis, then, answers the first key question of whether using software provides significant value to the customer.

## Skills and Resources

Now that AirEng has established its low-cost experiment's success criteria, you need to create a plan to execute the experiment. Given that your company probably doesn't have big-data analytics or artificial-intelligence expertise, it will need to partner with a firm that does have that expertise. Since such a partner firm will lack knowledge of AirEng's systems, AirEng will need to provide those experts and resources. The following list of skills and resources will be needed from within AirEng:

**Data architecture:** A data architect can help your team understand which data is being collected on engine performance and why, as well as what other associated internal hardware-related data might be available inside your organization. This person will also be responsible for interpreting the analysis that AirEng's partner software firm will help conduct. The data architect can also assess the relationship between different data points and the integrity of the data.

**Engineering:** Engineering skills will be required for any internal AirEng work that may arise. Engineers can determine what tools are required and can reconcile AirEng's engine road map and specifications.

**Business development and partnership:** Business development skills will be required to manage the selection of which software firm to partner with and to prepare the statement of work. Such a statement will detail the partner firm's role, deliverables, compensation, and schedule throughout the low-cost experiment.

**Legal:** A legal counsel will help manage the issues around data privacy and license agreements to ensure proper rights are in place for the collaboration between the software firm and AirEng and, potentially, with the customer, since the customer will provide engine data.

**Project management:** Given the project's multidisciplinary and multicompany nature, a dedicated project management role is required to plan, track, and execute the low-cost experiment within budget and on schedule. Ideally, the project manager will have some familiarity with managing software projects, which typically operate using agile methodologies rather than the long hardware cycles that AirEng project managers are used to. This is also a particularly important role in the incubation stage because much of the work to validate the critical assumptions will involve manual processes.

For example, the experiment team will collect data potentially from several departments at the customer's or AirEng's sites, clean up the data in preparation for analysis, and run numerous manual iterations on the analysis as insights are discovered along the way.

## Execution

AirEng's low-cost experiment execution can be broken into the following four phases (figure 6-1):

FIGURE 6-1

### AirEng's low-cost experiment

*Critical assumption:* Software can create significant incremental value over hardware sales, and customers will be willing to share that value.

*Low-cost experiment:* Build a low-cost visualization of a product's value proposition: software combined with hardware engine data and flight performance data can (1) accurately assess an engine's need for maintenance and (2) determine if a meaningful number of engines require maintenance less frequently.

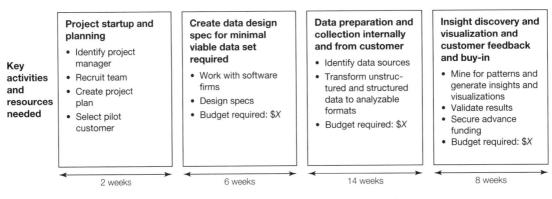

**Timeline (approximately 7.5 months total)**

**Success metrics:**
- Clear relationship between flight performance data and engine condition
- More than $X$ engines require maintenance less frequently
- More than $X$ value savings created, a greater reduction in spare engines required, and $X$ advance payment for condition-based service
- Line of sight to adding more features and instrumentation and to connecting with customer systems to eventually automate process for condition-based service

1. Identify the project manager, recruit team, and select a customer. The project manager will recruit an internal team to fill in the aforementioned skills that the project requires. The team will then need about two weeks to create a high-level project plan for the low-cost experiment, which will include the test customer to engage with and the estimated funding needed for the experiment. In this phase, the team must scope the experiment properly by precisely identifying what areas of engine maintenance will be explored. It must also obtain both the necessary approvals on those use cases and the funding for the low-cost experiment.

2. Focus on quickly identifying and partnering with a software firm with the relevant expertise and jointly creating a specification for data design. This data-design document should spell out the data that the project needs from both the customer and AirEng, the formats that the data needs to be in, and the steps that will be undertaken to clean the data or validate its integrity. If possible, AirEng will engage stakeholders—data architect counterparts at the customer—early. For instance, the data may need to be pulled in from relational databases or custom in-house data systems or simple text files, such as data logs. The earlier AirEng knows about the diversity and disparity of data sources, the better. Tactically, to partner with the software firm, the business development person will work with various stakeholders, such as the legal counsel and data architect, to draw up a contract that articulates the scope of the project, the compensation, the schedule, and the deliverables on each side. AirEng may estimate that this whole phase will be completed in, say, six weeks.

3. Prepare and collect data internally and from the customer. The third phase is the most intensive phase of the project. You need to collect the data from various departments at the customer and at AirEng, according to the data-design document, cleaning up the

data, and transforming it to the right formats to be amenable for analysis by the software firm. Given multiple dependencies, this phase could be a longer process, say, fourteen weeks.

4. Generate insights from the data, and get customer feedback and buy-in. The software firm may have to manually combine internal and external data, mine for patterns, and generate insights and visualizations. After the software firm iterates its analyses with feedback from AirEng, your team will need to interpret the insights and translate them to cost savings. In addition, the project manager will have to determine the additional costs of automating the savings and gain some confidence on the viability of this new revenue stream. The project manager will also partner with AirEng's customer-account manager or salesperson to then pitch the proposal to the customer. Together, they will push for a commitment for a deposit, predict the condition of engines, and offer a "condition-based service." This phase could take approximately eight weeks.

## Wrap-Up

Since your critical assumptions form the foundation of your Box 3 ideas, you have to test them for their validity.

- The incubation stage is intended to test critical assumptions at a low cost to reach a go/no-go decision on the Box 3 idea.

- Critical assumptions are those that, if proven wrong, are fatal to the success of the project.

- Most critical assumptions at this stage are usually customer-centric.

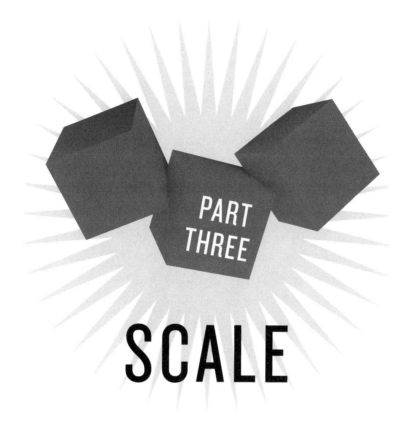

PART
THREE

# SCALE

U nlike ideation, which is fun, creative, and free of constraints, scaling is rife with obstacles and other challenges. It requires grit, dealing with ambiguity, and constant adaptation.

Scaling Box 3 ideas is difficult even if companies can see potential disruptions. But it is absolutely essential. Ideas, even great ones, can only get you so far. You need to execute.

Consider the equation for performance in Box 3:

Breakthrough innovation performance
= breakthrough ideas × breakthrough execution.

When we ask companies where they would rate themselves on break-through ideas on a scale of 1 (low) to 10 (high), they usually rate themselves as a 6. When we ask them where they rate themselves on execution using the same scale, the companies typically rate themselves as a 3. Thus, on average,

Performance = 6 × 3 = 18 units.

# SIEBEL SYSTEMS AND ITS STRUGGLE TO SCALE BOX 3

Siebel Systems, founded in 1993, began as a producer of sales-force automation software and later expanded into marketing and customer relationship management (CRM). By 1996, it was a publicly traded company. In 1999, *Fortune* magazine rated Siebel Systems the fastest-growing company in the United States.

Siebel aimed to serve the large-enterprise market with the company's complex, premium-priced products through an expensive direct-sales team. During the dot-com era, portals such as Salesforce.com began catering to small and medium-sized businesses that were cost-conscious and willing to adopt "good enough" products. In the software licensing model, licenses were given on a per-seat basis, where each seat is an individual with access to the product or service. Salesforce's average seat count was twenty-four per customer; Siebel's was one thousand per customer.

Siebel recognized the weak signals and the shift happening in the marketplace. In February 1999, the company launched Sales.com, a web-based sales-force automation product, in an effort to move downstream to the small and medium-sized businesses. Sales.com was a Box 3 move for the company. Within ten months of the launch, Siebel spun out Sales.com, funding it in partnership with Sequoia Capital and U.S. Venture Partners. As an independent company, Sales.com didn't borrow any of Siebel's capabilities and therefore couldn't leverage them.

However, in the second half of 2000, Siebel brought the independent company back inside with the intent of attracting cost-conscious customers to Sales.com and then nudging them to

---

When trying to improve innovation performance, companies find it easiest to go back to the drawing board and brainstorm better ideas. They might be able to ramp up their ideas to an 8. In this case,

Performance = 8 × 3 = 24 units.

Instead, if companies could raise their game on execution by just 2 units, the results would be more significant:

Performance = 6 × 5 = 30 units.

pricier Siebel products, leveraging Siebel's technology and sales force to do the nudging. Thus, the purpose of Box 3 was to serve the Box 1 business model. In practice, Sales.com was viewed as a threat to the core business. Analysts wondered why anyone would need Siebel's products if Sales.com's products were good enough. And yet, the setup was that Sales.com would not own its customers in the long term. Siebel's logic ignored the market's need for the Box 3 idea.

In April 2001, Siebel shut down Sales.com, citing the newer venture's limited ability to bring in customers for Siebel's enterprise products. Meanwhile, Siebel's competitor Salesforce.com continued to grow, showing that there was in fact a market for a Box 3 business model. Around the same time, the market entered a recession and Siebel's customers put CRM projects on indefinite hold. Staff on those projects were reassigned or let go. Siebel's reliance on the telecom sector had hurt the company. The recessionary environment meant there were fewer IT workers who could install Siebel software. Meanwhile, Salesforce.com's offering, which required few or no IT workers and employed nimble telemarketing teams, flourished in the small- and medium-business market.

*Source*: Bruce Cleveland, "Lessons from the Death of a Tech Goliath," *Fortune,* January 23, 2014, http://fortune .com/2014/01/23/lessons-from-the-death-of-a-tech-goliath; "Siebel to Shut Sales.com and Stress Direct License Sales," Gartner.com, May 2, 2001; Lisa DiCarlo, "Siebel to Buy Back Sales.com," *Forbes*, October 24, 2000, www .forbes.com/2000/10/24/1024siebel.html#2db0c7592012; Dave Kellogg, "Is Salesforce/Siebel a Classic Disruption Case?," *Kellblog* (blog), January 25, 2014, https://kellblog.com/2014/01/25/is-salesforce-siebel-a-classic-disruption-case-or-not.

Box 3 execution is difficult because it's different from Box 1 execution. The Box 1 performance engine is great at creating linear innovations. For a car manufacturer, for example, the talent, processes, and systems help it design engines and create new models each year. However, this dominant logic can be a significant liability when it comes to nonlinear innovations—say, creating mobility as a service à la Uber.

To scale Box 3 innovations, you'll need new talent, processes, and systems while also preserving Box 1's dominant logic. You'll have to consciously focus on overcoming three challenges, which we'll cover in detail.

**Forget:** The forget challenge is all about Box 2—selectively forgetting the past. Given how Box 3 execution differs from Box 1 execution, such ingredients as processes, methodologies, measurement metrics, and business-model assumptions that are still relevant drivers for Box 1's future growth must be forgotten by the Box 3 team. Instead, the team needs to overcome organizational inertia and develop a new culture and DNA to execute the Box 3 innovation.

**Borrow:** The borrow challenge is about which Box 1 assets Box 3 should borrow for its success. One common reason for failure in scaling Box 3 projects is a lack of partnership between Box 1 and Box 3 teams. Conflicts arise because the two teams have different jobs to do. Tensions, when ignored, quickly turn into hostilities, which, if not resolved, further degrade to outright warfare.

**Learn:** To scale up and deliver profits back to the company, the Box 3 project has to master a long and uncertain road, given that every innovation project is inherently risky. The learn challenge is to convert assumptions into knowledge efficiently, without spending excessive resources, and course-correct along the way. "Learning first, profits second" is the mantra that the organization must adopt. This approach requires a new mind-set from the Box 3 team as well as the leaders evaluating the team.

# 7

# FORGET

Managers running the Box 1 performance engine develop strong ideas about their customers, value proposition, and value-chain delivery mechanisms—and these ideas get embedded in systems, structures, and cultures. Such deep-rooted memory may be great for preservation (a feature of Box 1), but if it is not tamed sufficiently (an aspect of Box 2), it gets in the way of creation (Box 3). That's why Box 3 needs to forget the dominant logic of Box 1.

## Setting Up Your Team

To overcome the forget challenge, you'll set up a dedicated team that is solely responsible for scaling your Box 3 initiatives. You'll also often leverage some capabilities from Box 1.

## The Dedicated Team

Since Box 3 requires new competencies, the team dedicated to Box 3 should recruit new people and develop its own processes, systems, and structures, all of which should differ from those of the performance engine. The extent to which your dedicated team distinguishes itself from the performance engine will depend on the size of your forget challenge. New York Times Digital, for example, had to hire new talent that didn't exist on the print side—software engineers. Those were external hires.

## The Shared Staff

Often you can use some skills from the performance engine for Box 3 work. That is, some people can be shared between Box 1 and Box 3 initiatives. We call these resources *shared staff*.

Integration can be tricky. Shared staff can do more of the same work they already do, but might be unable to do different work. How different is *too different*? If it takes more than a few days' training to get the shared staff up to speed, then the work is too different. If it doesn't naturally fit into existing work processes, then it is too different. If the members of the shared staff can't stay in their current roles as currently defined and need to reorganize, develop new collaborations, or work at two different tempos, then the work is too different.

Companies sometimes ask too much of their shared staff, partly because of this group's aptitude. Not only are these individuals talented, but they also have a fantastic track record for execution. Therefore, companies imagine that this group can do everything, ignoring the limitations of the performance engine. For the shared staff, constructed for a specific purpose, the strength of the team is less than the sum of the individuals on the team. You may have heard that a team's strength is greater than the sum of the individuals. But the shared-staff members already have a job to do in Box 1. They can't break those constraints.

## Integration

When different teams are working together, you need to keep in mind people's roles and responsibilities to ensure that integration goes smoothly and produces results. Pay attention to the following distinctions:

- The Box 3 innovation team is the dedicated team (which is a distinct entity) *in partnership* with the shared staff (which is inside the performance engine).

- The dedicated team consists of people who are committed to the Box 3 project full-time. The shared staff works on the Box 3 project part-time.

- Because the shared staff remain inside the performance engine, these individuals operate according to the rules of the dominant logic. Little wonder there will be conflicts when shared staff are asked to collaborate with the Box 3 dedicated team.

## Arranging the Division of Work

In deciding on the division of work between the Box 1 performance engine and the Box 3 dedicated team, you will assess the teams on three critical dimensions: depth, power balance, and operating rhythm. Let's look at these in the context of Deere & Company, a US corporation that manufactures agricultural, construction, and forestry machinery. This discussion is based on ideas in *The Other Side of Innovation*, as quoted in a *Business Standard* article titled "Executing Innovation."[1]

**Depth:** Work relationships, or workflows, are the combination of skills used to get work done. They form as individuals habitually work together a certain way. In Deere's product development organization, the relationship between teams mirrors the product architecture. Wherever there is a mechanical, an electrical, or a spatial connection between components in, for example, a tractor, there is a work relationship between specialists in the product development organization. Thus, if Deere intends to launch a new product with a fundamentally new architecture, then the work relationships required between specialists will change. In such cases, individuals performing those workflows need to move to the dedicated team. In other words, if executing the Box 3 initiative requires a group of individuals to develop a new in-depth work relationship, this connection needs to happen within the confines of the dedicated team.

**Power balance:** Power balance refers to which individuals and groups are the most powerful. For instance, in Deere's organization, the power balance in work relationships is heavily shaped by customer priorities. Specialists instrumental in delivering on a critical customer need are more powerful than those who do not. Because Deere's customers care so deeply about reliability, there is a heavy complement of quality and reliability experts, and they are influential. Thus, if a new value proposition is offered to customers, where, for example, performance becomes more critical than reliability, the power balance will shift accordingly. If executing Box 3 shifts the power balance toward the individuals in the performance engine, then the work performed by these individuals must be assigned to the dedicated team.

**Operating rhythm:** Work relationships that cater to long, multiyear cycles will have a different operating rhythm than will work relationships that cater to short releases. In Deere's case, new tractor models are infrequently introduced, and therefore interactions among the product development team members are tuned to a long-term rhythm. Thus, if an add-on subscription

## HOW BMW USED A DEDICATED TEAM

When BMW faced an engineering challenge requiring a system-level design modification, the automaker created a dedicated team. The challenge was to create a hybrid automobile with a new technology, called regenerative braking. Traditional brakes dissipate a vehicle's energy of motion through friction, producing useless heat. Regenerative brakes capture and reuse that wasted energy. An electrical generator built into the brakes recharges the batteries as the car slows. While the engineers at BMW were definitely competent in designing this new technology, the established design processes were not fit for the task. Traditionally, there was no reason for battery specialists to interact with brake specialists, because the two components were unrelated. Thus, to build regenerative brakes, the performance engine would have to do not only more work but also different work, adding extra collaboration between the brake specialists and the battery specialists. BMW thus created a dedicated team to develop a regenerative braking system. The team was made up of brake specialists, battery specialists, and engine-control specialists for their first-ever close collaboration.

service with monthly releases is required, the required operating rhythm will change. If some of the Box 3 innovation work proceeds at a rhythm much different from that needed for performance-engine work, then this work should be done in the dedicated team.

# PROCESS

To build a dedicated team, you'll first access the magnitude of your forget challenge. Doing so will help you decide what new capabilities you need and what resources and talent to use from Box 1.

## Assessing the Magnitude of Your Forget Challenge

While every Box 3 experiment faces a difficult forget challenge, the intensity of this challenge depends on how different the Box 3 business model is from Box 1. The following three steps help explain the magnitude of the forget challenge you'll face.

**Step 1:** Compare the business models of Box 1 and Box 3.

| | Box 1 (performance engine) | Box 3 (experiment) |
|---|---|---|
| Customer | | |
| Value proposition | | |
| Value chain | | |
| Competencies | | |

**Step 2:** Assess the drivers of the forget challenge: unfamiliar customers, different value proposition, different processes, new competencies, different competitors, and significant market uncertainties. For the following statements, rate your responses on a numerical scale, where 1

means "strongly disagree" and 7 means "strongly agree." Write "NA" if the statement is not applicable to your situation:

| Statement | Rating |
|---|---|
| 1. Box 3 serves an unfamiliar customer. | |
| 2. Box 3 offers a fundamentally different value proposition. | |
| 3. Box 3 requires fundamentally different processes in various functions (sales, marketing, manufacturing, etc.). | |
| 4. Box 3 requires new competencies. | |
| 5. Box 3 has a different set of competitors. | |
| 6. Box 3 faces significant uncertainties; customer desires, technology, and competitors' behavior are evolving quickly and are difficult to predict. | |
| Average: | |

Now calculate the average rating (excluding NAs) to determine the magnitude of the fundamental drivers of the forget challenge. A score of 4 defines the midpoint between "low" and "high."

**Step 3:** Assess whether your company characteristics will intensify the forget challenge. As above, rate your responses to the following statements on a numerical scale, where 1 means "strongly disagree" and 7 means "strongly agree." Write "NA" if the statement is not applicable to your situation:

| Statement | Rating |
|---|---|
| 1. We primarily promote from within. | |
| 2. We have a homogeneous culture. | |
| 3. We have a strong culture. | |
| 4. Our employees have a long tenure in the company. | |
| 5. Other than entry-level positions, we rarely hire from the outside. | |
| 6. Even when we hire outsiders, we have strong socialization mechanisms. | |
| 7. We have a long track record of success. | |
| 8. Our dominant logic is "Don't mess with success." | |
| 9. Our top management team has a long tenure in the company. | |
| 10. Our top management team has worked primarily in the industry in which we compete. | |
| 11. We rarely recruit from the outside into our top management team. | |
| 12. We have a strong performance focus that places a premium on meeting short-term financial goals. | |
| 13. Our company has only one business model. | |

Calculate the average rating (excluding NAs) to determine the magnitude of the intensifiers of the forget challenge. A score of 4 defines the midpoint between "low" and "high."

———

The magnitude and intensity of the forget challenge will determine your approach to the dedicated team. The higher the numbers, the more distinct the dedicated team should be from the performance-engine team.

## Finding the Necessary Skills

To develop your dedicated team, list the skills required to execute the Box 3 idea. In listing skills, be as granular as you need to be, to differentiate the presently available and unavailable skills in your Box 1 organization. For example, you may need to include both selling face-to-face and selling online if the Box 3 initiative requires both skills and if only one is available within your organization. Then, in the box below, indicate whether the skill sets are available within your Box 1 organization. You must acquire every skill listed as unavailable by hiring someone new to the dedicated team:

| Skill | Available? (Yes/No) |
|---|---|
| 1. | |
| 2. | |
| 3. | |
| 4. | |

*(continued)*

| Skill | Available? (Yes/No) |
|---|---|
| 5. | |
| 6. | |
| 7. | |
| 8. | |
| 9. | |
| 10. | |

Every skill you marked as unavailable (with an "N") should be included in the dedicated team. And even if the skills necessary for Box 3 are available in Box 1, they may sometimes need to be moved to the dedicated team as well—if the workflows or work relationships in the performance engine are not compatible with those required in Box 3. These workflows should be assessed on whether they meet the requirements for three dimensions: depth, power balance, and operating rhythm. Fill in the following chart for each workflow (work relationship):

| Description | Does workflow meet Box 3 requirement for the dimension? (Yes/No) | | |
| --- | --- | --- | --- |
| | Depth | Power balance | Operating rhythm |
| Workflow 1 | | | |
| Workflow 2 | | | |
| Workflow 3 | | | |

Next, do the build-versus-buy analysis for obtaining the skills required for the Box 3 dedicated team. You can get an intact team via mergers and acquisitions (M&A), hire internally to create the team organically, or do a combination of both. M&A can potentially help with faster time to market but poses the challenge of integrating two cultures. For example, in 2016, General Motors bought a forty-person company, Cruise Automation, to get access to key autonomous-vehicle technology skill sets. In 2017, Cruise announced that it would launch an autonomous taxi service in San Francisco by the end of 2019. By mid-2019 the company had grown to about 1,500 people, and had raised billions of dollars in cash from investors such as SoftBank and Honda. The challenge of launching a completely autonomous taxi service was still an uphill battle, however. It cancelled its launch plans and continued running expanded tests beyond autonomous vehicle technology itself, particularly related to service aspects. Former GM president Dan Ammann became the company's head in 2018 and Cruise's founder and the former CEO Kyle Vogt became the CTO.[2]

For this exercise, you'll want to collaborate with your corporate development (M&A) team, along with your finance and HR team members. The M&A team especially has the expertise for such an analysis. The three teams are likely to compare both scenarios—build versus buy—along the following vectors:

### Feasibility

- If you are going to *build*, is the desired talent available in adequate supply? If there is a talent shortage, such as experts in the particular industry, your internal pay scales and systems may be inadequate to lure in talent to build the team, even if you were to find them.

- If you are going to *buy*, are there one or more intact teams available to be acquired? To what extent do you already know them? Do they lead the industry in terms of technology or talent? Feasibility analysis should include considerations, among others, of acquisition integration, retaining key talent, and geographic proximity to the desired location of the dedicated team.

### Cost

- Do you want to spend the money at the outset (acquisition) or phase in your spending (build)?

- Including all costs, such as those for deal making and integration, which is the cheaper option?

### Time-to-market impact of each scenario

- Can you target your window of business opportunity with each scenario, or is one scenario better suited for a time-to-market advantage?

### Quality of the resulting team

- Will building a team internally or buying one create a world-class team? Or will a combination of both approaches do it? For instance, you can build a team internally, but you may not wind up as competitive as the acquisition targets you ultimately try to buy.

- How well will the team align with the desired capabilities and with the shared staff?

- Are these skill sets what your company needs, regardless of the outcome of this specific venture?

### Probability of success for each scenario

- You'll want to risk-adjust each scenario based on constraints.

One trap that managers fall into during the scale phase is to over-build the team. Even though the initiative has made it to the scale phase, you need to pace yourself. Keeping the team as lean as possible is the best approach. Hence, resist the temptation to hire too quickly or make larger acquisitions than needed. You still want to operate like a startup group by having the team you need for the next few quarters of execution.

# HOW SIEBEL SYSTEMS USED M&A TO ACQUIRE KEY SKILL SETS

Let us continue the story of Siebel. A few years after Siebel closed down Sales.com, the company realized it still needed a response to Salesforce.com. Siebel had been responding to the market by only playing in enterprise sales and ignoring the hosted online CRM market. This narrower strategy had led to an erosion in sales. Lacking online CRM expertise, Siebel acquired UpShot Corporation, a leader in its market segment. UpShot had more training and implementation expertise than its competitors did. The acquired company brought new and different customers to Siebel. UpShot's customers welcomed the move as well. Since Siebel was a much larger company, it provided long-term stability, which UpShot's customers wanted. There was also some customer overlap between the companies, indicating that some players wanted both Box 1 and Box 3 solutions. Thus, even after Siebel sold itself to Oracle, UpShot revenues continued to grow through its software-as-a-service model.

Finally, use the following checklist to ensure that your team has enough outsiders:

| Source | Percentage | Adjustment | Effective outsiders (%) |
|---|---|---|---|
| Inside the company | | None | 0 |
| Inside the company but from a distinct and unrelated, or only loosely related, business unit | | Divide by 2 | |
| Outside the company | | None | |
| **Totals** | **100** | **None** | |

## THREE COMMON MISTAKES IN TEAM BUILDING

When building your dedicated team, make sure to avoid these common traps:

*Hiring only from within:* It's a common practice to move high performers from Box 1 to Box 3. But, depending on the capabilities you need, this move may not be appropriate. Having too many insiders may add to the significance of your forget challenge. Though it's OK to hire insiders, the leader of the Box 3 experiment should come from the outside. Why? An outsider has the positional power to challenge the status quo.

*Asking the performance engine to execute Box 3 innovation:* Given that the performance engine is not constructed for that objective, forgetting becomes an extremely difficult challenge.

*Using the same Box 1 performance metrics for Box 3 projects:* Box 3 is a business-model innovation. Therefore, it requires new performance metrics. For example, in a previous chapter, we discussed how GE, which sold $20,000 ECG machines in its performance engine, executed a Box 3 innovation by creating a $500 ECG machine to convert non-consumers to consumers in emerging markets. The more expensive machines are a premium-price, high-gross-margin business. If you applied the same constraints of high gross margins to the less expensive machine, the business would have been unlikely to take off, because the simpler machine is a low-margin, high-volume business. Thus, you must differentiate the performance metrics.

# IDEAS IN PRACTICE

In 1995, the NYTimes recruited Martin Nisenholtz to head the New York Times Digital Box 3 experiment. Nisenholtz had spent his entire career in interactive media, but he had little newspaper publishing experience. At the time, this hire was a very big deal for the NYTimes. Historically it wasn't common practice to hire from the outside. But in this case, since the company's Box 3 idea required new capabilities, it made sense to hire someone who wasn't bound by the company's dominant logic.

Nisenholtz was given a fairly high position, reporting to both the general manager and the editor of the *New York Times* newspaper. Furthermore, because of the strategic importance of NYTD, he was assigned a team of experienced *New York Times* newspaper journalists and IT staff (figure 7-1).

Unfortunately, with this structure, NYTD struggled for the next few years, because while Nisenholtz was a capable outsider, he was sandwiched between the top brass and the front line by dominant logic. The problem was simply that the organization asked the Box 1 structure, which was designed for a different business model, to execute a Box 3 idea.

As we have underscored, the struggle does not say anything about the quality of the individuals. In fact, as we have discussed, the *New York Times* had world-class journalists and other staff. However, those highly competent people were dedicated to a different objective. The *Times* newspaper is a known and understood system. The Box 1 team works hard to improve the newspaper, albeit incrementally. But the introduc-

**FIGURE 7-1**

**Martin Nisenholtz's original position in NYTimes hierarchy**

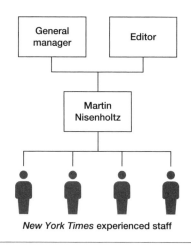

*New York Times* experienced staff

tion of a highly uncertain and nonroutine Box 3 project in that system led to major difficulties.

Furthermore, the *New York Times* company considered itself a newspaper business. However, NYTD is not a newspaper business but a technology business that happens to supply news, just as Google is a technology company that also provides news, among other things.

There were other issues as well. Nisenholtz's boss, the general manager of the printed newspaper, was evaluated on short-term financial results. Investing in NYTD would reduce short-term financial results because the payback would be far into the future. Therefore, if you make a Box 3 project a line item in Box 1's profit-and-loss statement, the project will always starve for the necessary investments. In fact, the printed newspaper's general manager could see NYTD as a threat because the new product could cannibalize revenues—both advertisements and subscriptions—from the *New York Times* newspaper. Thus, an insider could even have an active interest in killing the Box 3 project.

Thankfully, the top brass at the NYTimes realized the company needed to change. Now, let's see how the NYTimes would have accessed the magnitude of its forget challenge and formed a dedicated team. The following table shows how it could have compared its Box 1 and Box 3 business models:

| | Box 1 (performance engine: the *New York Times*) | Box 3 (experiment: NYTD) |
|---|---|---|
| **Customer** | • Primarily in the United States<br>• Advertisers, *Fortune* 500 companies | • Global<br>• Initial advertisers, other internet companies |
| **Value proposition** | • Daily news cycle<br>• Text and pictures<br>• Premium subscriptions<br>• Brand advertising | • Continuous news<br>• Multimedia<br>• Free<br>• Precise, targeted advertising |
| **Value chain** | • Analog | • Digital |
| **Competencies** | • Journalism expertise | • Software expertise |

Next, using our methods, the company would have assessed the main drivers of the forget challenge by rating the following statements on a numerical scale (1 = "strongly disagree"; 7 = "strongly agree"; NA = not applicable):

| Statement about Box 3 | Rating |
|---|---|
| 1. It serves an unfamiliar customer. | 5 |
| 2. It offers a fundamentally different value proposition. | 5 |
| 3. It requires fundamentally different processes in various functions (sales, marketing, manufacturing, etc.). | 7 |
| 4. It requires new competencies. | 3 |
| 5. It has a different set of competitors. | 5 |
| 6. It faces significant uncertainties. Customer desires, technology, and competitors' behavior are evolving quickly and are difficult to predict. | 7 |
| **Average:** | **5.3** |

The average rating (excluding NAs) signifies the magnitude of the fundamental drivers of the forget challenge. Since a score of 4 defines the midpoint between "low" and "high," the NYTimes Box 3 score of 5.3 skews toward a higher magnitude.

Finally, the company would have assessed the intensifiers of the forget challenge by rating the following statements on a numerical scale (1 = "strongly disagree"; 7 = "strongly agree"; NA = not applicable):

| Statement | Rating |
|---|---|
| 1. We primarily promote from within. | 7 |
| 2. We have a homogeneous culture. | 6 |
| 3. We have a strong culture. | 6 |

| Statement | Rating |
|---|---|
| 4. Our employees have a long tenure in the company. | 6 |
| 5. Other than entry-level positions, we rarely hire from the outside. | 6 |
| 6. Even when we hire outsiders, we have strong socialization mechanisms. | 6 |
| 7. We have a long track record of success. | 7 |
| 8. Our dominant logic is "Don't mess with success." | 7 |
| 9. Our top management team has a long tenure in the company. | 7 |
| 10. Our top management team has worked primarily in the industry in which we compete. | 7 |
| 11. We rarely recruit from the outside into our top management team. | 7 |
| 12. We have a strong performance focus that places a premium on meeting short-term financial goals. | 5 |
| 13. Our company has only one business model. | 4 |
| **Average:** | **6.2** |

The average rating (excluding NAs) signifies the magnitude of the intensifiers of the forget challenge. The company's score of 6.2 is fairly high. And since it scored high on both intensifiers and drivers, the forget challenge was large, if not daunting—which makes the company's transformation more remarkable.

## The Team

In 1998, the CEO of the NYTimes made some very bold moves. The executive restructured the organization so that Nisenholtz was promoted on the organizational chart, reporting directly to the corporate president and becoming a peer of the print newspaper's general manager (figure 7-2).

FIGURE 7-2

**Martin Nisenholtz's position in NYTimes hierarchy after restructuring**

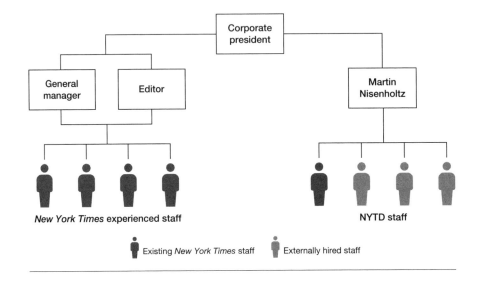

*New York Times* experienced staff        NYTD staff

Existing *New York Times* staff     Externally hired staff

Think about how difficult a decision this might have been for the CEO, given that the bulk of the revenues were then coming from the printed newspaper. At best, NYTD was a small operation losing money. Yet on the organizational chart, both Nisenholtz and the newspaper's general manager were reporting as peers to the corporate president. Furthermore, Nisenholtz was told to construct a team that was capable of implementing an internet media business and that he need not be constrained by the rules by which the newspaper business operated.

As a first step in building a dedicated team, Nisenholtz had to list the skills he knew would be necessary for the NYTD project. He then had to see which of the skills were available within the company and which would need to be sourced from outside the NYTimes. He might have created a table something like the following:

| Skill | Available? |
| --- | --- |
| Leadership skills (experience leading an online digital initiative) | No |
| Online consumer market research | No |
| Project or program management | Yes |
| Content management | Yes |
| Front-end development (e.g., JavaScript programming skills, user interface skills) (Note: software skills may be available in Box 1's IT staff but not necessarily an individual with UI or JavaScript skills) | No |
| Search engine optimization | No |
| Online advertising | No |
| Back-end development (e.g., SQL programming skills) | No |
| Software-build management | No |
| Software development (e.g., C programming language skills) | No |
| Online marketing | No |
| Operations management | Yes |
| Finance | Yes |
| Software testing (front-end, back-end, and development testing) | No |
| Performance testing (e.g., testing how fast the page loads) | No |
| Web analytics | No |
| Legal (end-user license agreement) | No |
| Affiliate marketing | No |
| Server management and administration (e.g., where content will be hosted) | No |
| Online customer-support community or newsgroup | No |
| Online partnerships | No |
| Continuous planning, triage, and updates (24-7 newsbreak monitoring) | No |
| User experience and graphic designers | Yes |
| Privacy and security experts | No |
| Information technology (IT) | Yes |

Within one year, the NYTD staff had grown to approximately four hundred employees, 75 percent of whom were hired from the outside. The outside hires had software, not newspaper, expertise. One of the core competencies of NYTD is software. The software engineers that NYTD hired were generally younger than the *New York Times* staff and were compensated differently. After all, a software engineer in Silicon Valley faces a different labor market than that faced by a traditional newspaper staff member and must be compensated accordingly.

Nisenholtz was also given complete freedom to change processes. For instance, a new product introduction in the *New York Times* newspaper implied adding a new section to the newspaper. The process took several years and careful research. In the NYTD world, however, new products had to be constantly tested and improved on quickly. Therefore, Nisenholtz created a new process that was much more flexible, more agile, and shorter.

Nisenholtz was allowed to change his performance metrics and planning processes as well as his group's culture. NYTD moved into a new building in Midtown Manhattan, about ten blocks from the newspaper's headquarters. The design of the new workspace was meant to reinforce NYTD's new culture. The area looked modern, much different from corporate headquarters. There were large, open spaces and "teaming" areas, including a central café, to encourage conversation and cooperation. The senior executives had glass-walled offices to enhance the sense of openness. The layout was meant to be much more collaborative to serve the needs of NYTD, and it paved the way to a different culture.

## Wrap-Up

In scaling your Box 3 project, you must recognize that Box 1 and Box 2 can pose challenges to your innovation efforts. This chapter discussed how these three areas differ:

- To successfully execute linear innovations inside the Box 1 performance engine, companies develop a dominant logic—the kind of people recruited, the capabilities they build, the processes they use, the performance metrics they deploy, and so forth.

- Because a Box 3 experiment is a nonlinear innovation and therefore faces a Box 2 challenge, it must forget the dominant logic.

- You need to create a dedicated team for Box 3 that is separate from the performance engine, with different capabilities, different processes, and different performance metrics.

# 8

# BORROW

The borrow challenge is figuring out how many of Box 1's assets you must use for Box 3's success, how to optimally structure the talent and resources across both boxes, and, given the conflicts and trade-offs involved, how to successfully manage the links.

There must be some assets that Box 3 can leverage from Box 1. After all, the question is, Why would the initiative succeed within the company instead of outside of it? For example, consider that assets from the *New York Times* benefited NYTD—brand, content, and relationships with advertising. These are assets that no Silicon Valley startup can compete with.

However, when assets from the performance engine go to benefit Box 3, significant conflicts are likely to arise.

## Anticipating Potential Conflicts

Suppose you have a common sales force that is selling advertising for both the *New York Times* newspaper and NYTD. This shared staffing could raise several conflicts.

For example, the sales force might not have time to sell NYTD's advertisements. Maybe you assumed the sales force has 10 percent slack, but in practice it doesn't. Now you've asked the salespeople to do two jobs when earlier they were doing just one job. The sales force is overworked and unlikely to help Box 3.

But let's assume the sales force does indeed have 10 percent slack and that this is all that's needed to support Box 3 advertisement sales for NYTD. Looking closely, you'll see that this 10 percent slack is not evenly distributed throughout the day. It is entirely possible that the moment Box 3 requests time from the sales force is the moment the staff members are 100 percent busy. Hence, they cannot cooperate with the Box 3 request.

A third conflict is the fear of cannibalization. Sales reps may be afraid that opening the door for a *Fortune* 500 company to advertise in NYTD, when that company currently advertises with the printed newspaper, will cannibalize sales. The fear is greatest when there is a very high margin with that *Fortune* 500 company's full-page printed ad.

Finally, consider a scenario in which Box 3 is scaling splendidly. But unfortunately, the shared staff members from Box 1 are pushing back because they have no way to execute to their own Box 1 successful outcome. Through the shared arrangement, Box 1 has been shortchanged on talent. In fact, the more successful Box 3 becomes, the greater the conflicts.

There can be all kinds of conflicts—for resources, time, management attention, and so forth. These conflicts are real and legitimate. They will happen because of the shared nature of borrowed resources (figure 8-1).

If you ignore the conflicts that begin with minor tensions, they will turn into major rivalries. If you ignore the major rivalries between Box 1 and Box 3, those rivalries will ramp up to significant hostilities. And ignoring those hostilities will turn into outright warfare.

FIGURE 8-1

**The innovation team: The partnership between the Box 1 shared staff and the Box 3 dedicated team**

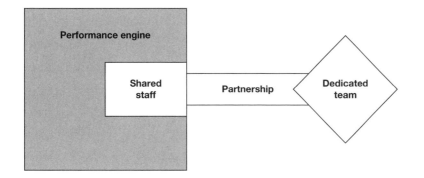

In a tug-of-war between the small dedicated team and the huge performance engine, the dedicated team will lose every time. Why? There are more people in the performance engine, and it is a powerful force to reckon with, particularly given that it brings in near-term profits.

However, if you can foster a healthy partnership between Box 1 and Box 3, the picture changes. How do you cultivate this partnership? That is the essence of the *borrow* challenge. There are three common mistakes to avoid if you want to build a healthy partnership.

## Borrowing Too Much

A rule of thumb is that the performance engine should lend no more than three assets to Box 3 initiatives. The question you must ask is, What *strategic assets* are a must for Box 3 to borrow from Box 1? For instance, cost reduction is not a reason to create a borrowing link between Boxes 1 and 3. Whatever Box 3 borrows must have a strategic advantage, as every borrowing relationship creates conflicts. Thus, borrowing relationships must be kept to a bare minimum. That said, Box 3 must not be totally isolated, with no borrowing from Box 1.

## Ignoring the Performance Engine's Legitimate Concerns

There are three types of legitimate concerns the performance engine might express. First, Box 1 might complain and ask for additional resources to help the Box 3 project. This request could be a legitimate concern since you are asking Box 1 to do *more* work. In such cases, it is advisable to give the Box 1 performance engine additional resources.

Second, the performance engine might complain that it has not been given the right incentives. For instance, if there is a common sales force between Box 1 and Box 3, the sales staff is less likely to devote time to Box 3 if the sales commission is the same for all products. Selling Box 3 products requires more time and effort since it involves new customers and new value propositions. You can address this disparity by offering a special commission to the common sales force to sell Box 3 products. Another way to redesign incentives is to have the Box 3 dedicated team pay for what it gets from the shared staff by establishing a transfer price. In this scenario, the performance engine views the dedicated team more as a customer than as a partner.

Third, it is not uncommon for the Box 3 leader or team members to come across as condescending toward Box 1 because Box 3 usually is the shiny new object getting management's attention. One way to mitigate such conflicts is to choose a dedicated team leader who demonstrates humility.

## Ignoring Tensions between the Performance Engine and the Dedicated Team

Even if you avoid the first two mistakes, you may still have conflicts. Therefore, avoid the third mistake, which is that if you are a CEO, you begin to ignore those conflicts, hoping Box 1 and Box 3 leaders are adults and can work it out themselves. Conflicts are real, and they can happen every day. CEOs must roll up their sleeves and get down to operational details to resolve conflicts. Here are some ways to resolve such conflicts:

- Include insiders on the dedicated team in roles that demand heavy coordination with the performance engine.

- Formally allocate resources for Box 3 projects through a unified budget for both the dedicated team and the shared staff.

- Actively adjudicate operational conflicts.

- Articulate strategic intent that includes both Box 1 and Box 3 in creating the future.

- Emphasize common and core values that apply to everyone and bind them together.

Avoiding the aforementioned common mistakes will ensure that you have a healthy partnership instead of a tug-of-war between the dedicated team, the shared staff, and the performance engine.

# PROCESS

To conquer the borrowing challenge, you'll want to set up a half-day to full-day meeting with the relevant Box 1 and Box 3 stakeholders, including the Box 1 and Box 3 leaders. Here, you'll look at potential conflicts from both a Box 1 and a Box 3 perspective, and you'll create mitigation strategies in advance. Finally, you'll use a checklist to ensure you are on the right track in terms of setting up a healthy partnership between Boxes 1 and 3.

## Setup

Here are some rules of thumb for the meeting.

- Make sure the attendees are cross-disciplinary—for example, engineering, sales, finance, manufacturing, and marketing representatives.

- Have a dinner or happy hour the night before the meeting so that people are familiar with each other.

- Distribute name tags with individuals' names and roles on the day of the meeting.

- Have people sit in diverse functional teams, encouraging those who don't know each other to sit together.

- Assign the role of a meeting scribe—someone who will capture the various discussions promptly in the meeting. This is a critical role, so make sure that whoever is assigned this role has good operational skills.

## Proposed Agenda

**Introduction (sixty minutes, including Q&A):** Open the meeting by having the Box 3 leader articulate Box 3's business plan so that all attendees, from Box 1 and Box 3, share the same foundational understanding. The presentation should include the context of why winning is important for the entire company.

**Team assembly:** Break the group into three teams, with each team including Box 1 and Box 3 members. Generally, about five members per team is ideal. If there are more members, feel free to create additional teams.

**Team task (about twenty minutes):** Each team should work on listing up to three Box 1 assets that give significant competitive advantage to Box 3. If you were the NYTimes, for example, those borrowed assets could be brand, advertising relationships, and content. Note: fewer assets is better, and stress that teams should list no more than three.

| Borrowed asset priority | Box 1 assets that Box 3 will borrow to gain significant competitive advantage |
|---|---|
| 1. | |
| 2. | |
| 3. | |

**Debrief (fifteen minutes):** Each team presents its list to all the others, highlighting why each borrowed asset can be leveraged for the benefit of Box 3. The Box 3 leader will pick the top one, two, or three assets to borrow.

**Team assignment:** At this time, assign team 1 to the first listed asset, and ensure that the team has an expert for this asset. For instance, if this asset 1 is *brand*, you need to have somebody from the brand team on team 1. Similarly, assign team 2 to asset 2, and so forth, making sure to have at least one domain expert pertaining to the assigned asset on each team.

**Hat switching (thirty minutes):** Have each team think about all the conflicts that may arise when those assets are borrowed. First, the entire team wears a virtual Box 1 hat to identify concerns or conflicts that Box 1 might have when the assets are borrowed. For instance, for brand, Box 1 might be concerned that the Box 3 experiment will harm its own brand's reputation.

| Borrowed asset | Potential concerns from Box 1's perspective |
|---|---|
|  |  |
|  |  |
|  |  |

Next, have the entire team wear a virtual Box 3 hat to identify concerns Box 3 might have regarding the assets it is borrowing.

| Borrowed asset | Potential concerns from Box 3's perspective |
|---|---|
|  |  |
|  |  |
|  |  |

**Debrief (twenty minutes each, for a total of sixty minutes for three teams):** Each team presents to the others the Box 1 and Box 3 anticipated conflicts for each of the borrowed assets. For example, the performance engine—the *New York Times* newspaper—might be concerned about any changes to the look and feel of the NYTD website that make it inconsistent with its *New York Times* brand positioning. One of the by-products of doing this exercise— wearing Box 1 and Box 3 hats at different times—in a mixed team of Box 1 and Box 3 individuals is that it enables each attendee to see the other group's perspective and not lock themselves into one way of thinking. This more open mind-set helps build the trust people need for managing conflicts when the teams have to work with each other.

**Resolution plan:** Finally, assign joint owners from Box 1 and Box 3 to look at the conflicts listed. Their job is to come up with mitigation or resolution strategies to manage the conflicts. Encourage them to come up with creative win-win solutions.

| Category | Box owners | Conflict description | Mitigation/resolution plan |
|----------|------------|----------------------|----------------------------|
| | Box 1:<br><br>Box 3: | | |
| | Box 1:<br><br>Box 3: | | |
| | Box 1:<br><br>Box 3: | | |

| Category | Box owners | Conflict description | Mitigation/resolution plan |
|---|---|---|---|
| | Box 1: | | |
| | Box 3: | | |
| | Box 1: | | |
| | Box 3: | | |

## Checklists

As leaders for the initiative—you and the general managers, the senior-most Box 1 and Box 3 members—will want to ensure that adequate actions have been taken to foster a healthy relationship between Box 1 and Box 3.

The three of you will do this in a number of ways while bringing along the team, as follows. If you notice that a checklist item hasn't been completed, then take the time to make sure it gets done by scheduling or resolving it in near future. First, make sure that resource allocations have been coordinated. To do this, list all performance-engine leaders who make formal and explicit resource allocations that affect your initiative. For example, the head of manufacturing makes explicit allocations to production capacity, choosing whether to manufacture performance-engine products or a new product that the Box 3 initiative is bringing to market.

| Performance-engine leader | Resource allocation decision |
|---|---|
| 1. | 1. |
| 2. | 2. |
| 3. | 3. |

Then, confirm that you have completed the following actions:

| Action | Completed? (Yes/No) |
|---|---|
| 1. We have included all resource allocations made by performance-engine leaders on the formally approved plan for the Box 3 initiative. | |
| 2. We have discussed possible conflicts and contingency plans (e.g., sudden growth or sudden decline of the innovation initiative) with each performance-engine leader *in advance*. | |
| 3. There exists a clear "appeals process" to resolve conflicts; it is adjudicated by the supervising executive. | |
| 4. Box 3 is paying for the explicit costs of what the shared staff provides (whether fully utilized or not) through an internal accounting transfer. | |
| 5. Arrangements have been made to correct the performance metrics of the performance-engine leader so that they are isolated from the (potentially negative) impact of the innovation initiative. | |

You also need to ensure that Box 3 gets sufficient time and energy from the shared staff. List below the groups of people (or functions) in the shared staff, and note the times they are under the greatest pressure to meet performance-engine imperatives. For example, you might note that salespeople are under extreme pressure to close deals at the end of the quarter:

| Group or function | Busiest times |
|---|---|
| 1. | 1. |
| 2. | 2. |
| 3. | 3. |

Does the shared staff have any fears about the Box 3 initiative?

| Potential fear | A shared-staff fear? (Yes/No) |
|---|---|
| It could cannibalize an existing product or service. | |
| It could make an existing process obsolete and put performance-engine jobs at risk. | |
| It could reduce or put at risk incentive compensation. | |
| It might damage a brand. | |

*(continued)*

| Potential fear | A shared-staff fear? (Yes/No) |
|---|---|
| It might damage a customer relationship. | |
| It might damage some other performance-engine asset. | |
| List any other potential fears: | |

Next, confirm that you have completed the following actions:

| Action | Completed? (Yes/No) |
|---|---|
| We have engaged the Box 1 supervising executive in actively promoting the importance of the initiative to the shared staff, especially during its busiest times. | |
| We have considered ways to minimize the burden on shared staff, especially during its busiest times. | |
| We have made the Box 1 supervising executive aware of any specific fears of the shared staff. | |
| This executive has been brought in to persuade the shared staff members that despite their fears, the innovation initiative is in the company's long-term best interest. | |
| We are paying for a reasonably approximated cost of the shared staff's time through internal accounting transfer. | |
| With Box 1's supervising executive, we have arranged for special targets or bonuses to motivate the shared staff to push the Box 3 initiative forward and to participate in the upside as Box 3 becomes successful. | |

Avoid disharmony in the partnership. Find out if the shared staff has any of the following resentments or unfavorable perceptions of the dedicated team:

| Perception | A shared-staff concern? (Yes/No) |
|---|---|
| The dedicated team feels superior to the rest of the company. | |
| The dedicated team thinks it is the most important group in the company. | |
| The dedicated team gets special treatment and is not held to the same standards of performance as the rest of the company. | |
| The dedicated team is paid too well. | |
| The dedicated team can't be trusted. | |
| The dedicated team thinks it is or should be in charge of everything. | |
| List any other resentments or unfavorable perceptions: | |

The following steps must also be taken to reduce the likelihood of toxic tensions between the dedicated team and the shared staff:

| Action | Completed? (Yes/No) |
|---|---|
| We have worked with the Box 1 supervising executive to discuss and mitigate the shared staff's resentments. The shared staff has a clear understanding of why the Box 3 initiative is in the company's long-term best interest, despite the short-term sacrifices. | |
| We are closely monitoring and eliminating any actions or behaviors of the dedicated team that may unnecessarily exacerbate any ill will from the shared staff. | |

*(continued)*

| Action | Completed? (Yes/No) |
|---|---|
| We have made the division of responsibilities between the dedicated team and shared staff very clear. | |
| We have strengthened common bonds by reinforcing the values and aspirations that both the dedicated team and the shared staff share. | |
| Where possible, we have chosen insiders for the dedicated-team roles that require the most interaction with the shared staff. | |
| We have tried to make it easy for the dedicated team and the shared staff to interact face-to-face. | |
| We have worked with the supervising executive to modify the individual performance evaluations of the shared staff and the dedicated team so that the evaluations explicitly address each individual's ability to collaborate with the other group. | |

# IDEAS IN PRACTICE

Let's imagine how the NYTimes would have conducted these exercises as it worked to build its successful Box 3 digital innovation, NYTD. The Box 3 team would have borrowed three assets from Box 1 to gain significant competitive advantage: brand, content, and advertising relationships.

Wearing their Box 1 hat, the team could have identified these concerns about the borrowed assets:

| Borrowed asset | Potential concerns from Box 1's perspective |
|---|---|
| Brand | Brand-promise erosion: The *New York Times* brand stands for a premium product. If the perceived quality of the Box 3 product is poor, it could affect the reputation of the *New York Times* printed newspaper, eventually driving down sales. |
| Content | Box 1 may want to prioritize publishing content in the printed newspaper. For instance, if Box 3 breaks the story, the digital action reduces the originality of the publication in the printed newspaper—originality that its customers have come to expect. Box 1 may also be concerned that Box 3 is prioritizing speed over following the necessary process to ensure that the story has been fact-checked prior to publishing. |
| Advertising relationships | Box 1 might be concerned that if Box 3 offers different and sweeter pricing terms than the print side offers to advertisers, the practice could lead the advertisers to demand the same terms from the printed newspaper, eventually driving down advertising prices there. |

And wearing their Box 3 hat, they would have identified these potential issues:

| Borrowed asset | Potential concerns from Box 3's perspective |
|---|---|
| Brand | Box 3 might be concerned that Box 1 will resist modifications to the brand's visual elements (e.g., colors and logos that match the user interface) that Box 3 needs to compete in the digital market. For instance, Box 3 might need to project a modern image, breaking away from the "old" newspaper look while still leveraging the *New York Times* brand name and equity.<br><br>Even if Box 1 agrees to the necessary changes, it needs to commit to doing additional work toward making the changes available by Box 3's deadlines. Box 3 may also worry that Box 1 will push back and will ask for additional resources or time. |
| Content | Box 3 may want to publish content as the story breaks rather than on a daily basis, as Box 1 is used to doing. Box 3 thus works to have Box 1 content available at different times and would like the freedom to operate at a near-real-time pace by breaking the story as it deems fit. |
| Advertising relationships | Given that Box 3 is virtually a startup, it may want to offer advertisers discounts to lure them to advertise on an unknown platform or offer other incentives, such as relaxed payments terms, which Box 1 would oppose.<br><br>Box 3 may be concerned that for various reasons (e.g., Box 1's lack of incentives and time and its fear of cannibalization), Box 1 will not give Box 3 enough attention from the sales and marketing teams to open doors at the top advertisers. |

To mitigate these issues, they could have come up with the following plans:

| Category | Box owners* | Conflict description | Mitigation/resolution plan |
|---|---|---|---|
| Brand | **Box 1:** Linda L., director, brand strategy<br><br>**Box 3:** Rush T., marketing director | Brand-promise erosion: The *New York Times* brand stands for a premium product. If the perceived quality of the Box 3 product is poor, it could affect the reputation of the *New York Times* printed newspaper, eventually driving down sales. | Quarterly brand measurements with survey questions to verify that Box 3 is not hurting Box 1. Agree on what exceptions Box 3 is allowed with respect to the brand-promise pillars of Box 1. |

*(continued)*

| Category | Box owners* | Conflict description | Mitigation/resolution plan |
|---|---|---|---|
| Content | **Box 1:** Jane P., executive editor, *New York Times*<br><br>**Box 3:** Martin N., executive editor, NYTD | Box 3 requires freedom to operate in building and releasing content on a real-time basis, with faster time-to-market and with different quality criteria than Box 1. | Limit borrowing to only those Box 1 stories that can be released on NYTD to coincide with Box 1 releases. Create a separate newsroom for Box 3 content with freedom to operate in alignment with its business needs. |
| Advertising relationships | **Box 1:** Joe M., sales director<br><br>**Box 3:** Rush T., marketing director | Given that Box 3 is virtually a startup, it may want to offer advertisers discounts to lure them to advertise on an unknown platform or offer other incentives, such as relaxed payments terms, which Box 1 would oppose. | Agree that Box 3 can offer discounts or other special terms to customers that are not currently advertising in the printed newspaper. Also agree that Box 3 can offer these terms to a specific list of Box 1 customers. |
| Advertising relationships | **Box 1:** Joe M., sales director<br><br>**Box 3:** Rush T., marketing director | Box 3 may be concerned that for various reasons (e.g., Box 1's lack of incentives and time and its fear of cannibalization), Box 1 will not give Box 3 enough attention from the sales and marketing teams to open doors at the top advertisers. | Double-count sales revenue—that is, advertising sales revenue on the online platform will be counted as revenues for both Box 3 and Box 1. This practice will provide incentives for Box 1 to open doors for selling Box 3. |

*The names in this table are made up.

# Wrap-Up

As a leader, you must strategically balance the potentially conflicting groups when you borrow necessary resources from your company's performance engine. A few key points of understanding can help you and your team better face the borrow challenge:

- The dedicated team, while distinct, cannot be entirely isolated from the performance engine. There are performance-engine assets that can be leveraged for the benefit of the dedicated team.

We call them shared staff, and they remain within the performance engine but are used by the dedicated team.

- The Box 3 innovation team is *not* the dedicated team but rather it is the dedicated team working in partnership with the shared staff.

- The dedicated team consists of people who work full-time on the Box 3 project, while the shared staff works part-time on it. Such an arrangement inevitably will create conflicts between the performance engine and the dedicated team. Anticipating and mitigating conflicts is job number one for the success of Box 3.

# 9

# LEARN

There are two types of acceptable outcomes in an innovation effort: (1) a success and (2) a failure that comes as quickly and inexpensively as possible. The most undesirable outcome is a long, expensive, painful failure. Therefore, as the Box 3 initiative moves forward, you want to spend a little to learn a lot and to reduce project risks. To do this, you need to test the critical assumptions (as described, assumptions that if proven incorrect would kill the project) using low-cost experiments and base your course of action on the experiments' outcome. Let's look at some ways to enhance this type of learning.

## Running a Disciplined Experiment

Executing a Box 3 project involves knowing how to run a *disciplined experiment*. Your ability to learn faster than your competition is your only sustainable competitive advantage. The best way to deliver financial results in Box 3 is not to focus on short-term financial criteria. Instead, you should use leading indicators to evaluate Box 3 experiments. The leading indicators provide signals about resolving the critical assumptions. That, ultimately, leads to financial success.

Here are the steps in a disciplined experiment:

1. Plan the experiment to test a hypothesis.

2. Predict what you think is going to happen, documenting as clearly as possible how you came up with your predictions.

3. Execute the experiment, collecting all relevant data.

4. Analyze your results. Specifically, compare what you thought was going to happen with what actually happened. It is through careful analysis of the differences between predictions and outcomes that you learn.

### Plan the Experiment

Every Box 3 project needs a special plan. Planning in Box 3 is very different from planning in Box 1, as the following table illustrates:

| Planning in Box 1 | Planning in Box 3 |
| --- | --- |
| Based on precedent | Start with a blank page |
| Emphasize data | Emphasize assumptions |
| Standard scorecard | Custom scorecard |
| Highlight quarterly and yearly totals | Highlight trends |
| Hold firm expectations | Adjust expectations often, based on actual results |
| Focus on results | Focus on learning |

Create a separate custom plan with custom metrics for each Box 3 initiative. Performance evaluation for Box 3 projects must take place in a forum different from Box 1 performance evaluations; the conversations are entirely different. When a performance engine falls behind plan, the conversation is all about how to get back on plan. When a Box 3 initiative falls behind plan, the conversation should prioritize the possibility that the plan was based on faulty assumptions.

In Box 3, the most important conversations center on two questions: What are we spending money on? And why?

Assume you are spending money on building a new business, called Product Reviews, which assesses and compares new products. Say it operates online and has an advertising-based business model. As you look at various categories of dollar spending, you may categorize them into the following buckets: market research, content, marketing, information technology, and sales. You can think about why you are incurring these expenditures and what outcomes you hope to achieve.

Consider marketing spending. To understand why you have certain marketing expenditures, you could create a list of desired outcomes, both operational and financial, such as increases in revenue, users on the website, pages viewed, and advertisements sold.

We now have our hypothesis in an if-then format. *If* there is marketing spending, *then* the number of users on the website increases.

## Make Predictions

You want to test this if-then causal relationship. The causal path from marketing spending to revenues can be illustrated as follows:

Marketing spending → Website users → Page views →
Ads sold → Revenues

## Run the Experiment and Collect Data

All the outcomes on the preceding causal map become potential metrics to monitor and measure. For metrics that are not directly measurable, we should identify a proxy, something closely correlated to the outcome of interest.

The metrics closest to the root of each chain are the *leading indicators*—results that will give the first alerts that the initiative is or is not on track. In the above example, it will be website users. Watch the leading indicators, and you will spend a little and learn a lot.

When monitoring, remember that trends matter more than the numbers themselves. Trends are important because innovation initiatives are dynamic and can get even worse *before* they get better. In this way, the value of the prediction is not in its accuracy but in its subsequent analysis for learning. All we want to know is, Are we on the trajectory to success?

### Analyze the Results

Obviously, if your outcome matches your prediction, you've succeeded. But if it doesn't match, there are four possible explanations:

1. The cause-and-effect relationship doesn't exist.

2. You haven't spent enough money to get the predicted impact.

3. You haven't waited long enough for the predicted impact.

4. Additional variables that you have not considered are affecting the desired outcomes.

We'll focus on the first explanation, which is the most complicated: the cause-and-effect relationship doesn't exist. If this is the case, it's time to change direction and test your critical assumptions.

To find those that are critical, first list all your assumptions, asking two questions about the cause-effect link: What is the likelihood that our conjecture about this cause-and-effect relationship is wrong? And if it is wrong, what are the consequences? Some of the links will be entirely speculative, while others are nearly certain, in light

FIGURE 9-1

**Identifying the most critical unknowns**

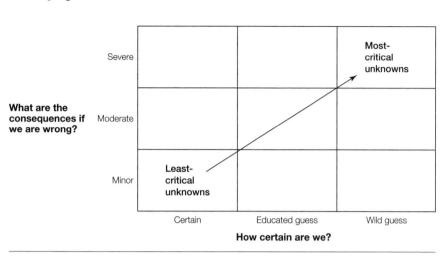

of experience in the established business. The implications of being wrong could range from trivial to disastrous. You should regard the assumptions that are both highly uncertain and highly consequential as the most critical ones (figure 9-1).

## Evaluating the Leadership and Learning

Finally, we cannot emphasize enough that the innovation leader must be evaluated subjectively. To do this, answer the following questions:

- Are the critical assumptions clear and well understood? Which are the most uncertain assumptions and the most consequential?

- Do changes in plans come out of data that supports a clear lesson learned?

- Is the innovation leader trying to learn quickly and cheaply?

- Is the innovation leader willing to face facts, even when those facts are unpleasant?

- Are predictions improving?

# PROCESS

To overcome the learn challenge, plan a meeting for an entire day or longer with key members of the Box 3 team. The attendees should be cross-functional to be able to help with assumptions centered on the market or customer, on development, and on monetization. Ask the leader to prepare a thirty-minute presentation to discuss the Box 3 experiment goals and key milestones twelve to eighteen months out.

## Preliminary Meeting

Break the group of attendees into three teams, with leaders assigned to each team. Call the teams customer-centric, development-centric, and monetization-centric. Assign to each team leaders who are functional experts in, and accountable for, those areas. The other members of the team should be cross-functional—from sales, finance, marketing, HR, and so on. If there are more team members, feel free to duplicate the teams. Print name tags for each participant, and order the accessories needed for the meeting, such as pens, markers, and a whiteboard or other marker boards.

A day or more before the meeting, distribute a handout of sample questions about critical assumptions that attendees should become familiar with before the meeting (see the appendix). They don't need to answer any of the questions yet. Inform them that they will work in pre-assigned teams to answer the questions.

# Meeting Day

The following agenda will give you an approximate format for how to allow time for each activity:

**Meeting introduction (0.5 hour):** Start the meeting with a thirty-minute summary to get everyone on the same page. Articulate the group's vision and key milestones that the leader or general manager hopes the team can achieve in the next twelve to eighteen month time frame.

**Discussion (1 hour):** Create a list of assumptions for Box 3.

**Analysis (0.5 hour):** Identify the critical assumptions. Using a scale of 1 to 5, rate each of the assumptions on its degree of uncertainty (1 = certain, 5 = wild guess) and the severity of consequence if you are wrong (1 = minor, 5 = severe). The assumptions with the highest total score are the most critical—those that you should test first.

| Assumption | Consequences if wrong | Certainty | Total of scores in columns 2 and 3 |
|---|---|---|---|
| 1. | | | |
| 2. | | | |

(continued)

| Assumption | Consequences if wrong | Certainty | Total of scores in columns 2 and 3 |
|---|---|---|---|
| 3. | | | |
| 4. | | | |
| 5. | | | |
| 6. | | | |
| 7. | | | |

| Assumption | Consequences if wrong | Certainty | Total of scores in columns 2 and 3 |
|---|---|---|---|
| 8. | | | |
| 9. | | | |
| 10. | | | |
| 11. | | | |
| 12. | | | |

(continued)

| Assumption | Consequences if wrong | Certainty | Total of scores in columns 2 and 3 |
|---|---|---|---|
| 13. | | | |
| 14. | | | |
| 15. | | | |
| 16. | | | |
| 17. | | | |

| Assumption | Consequences if wrong | Certainty | Total of scores in columns 2 and 3 |
|---|---|---|---|
| 18. | | | |
| 19. | | | |
| 20. | | | |
| 21. | | | |
| 22. | | | |

(continued)

| Assumption | Consequences if wrong | Certainty | Total of scores in columns 2 and 3 |
|---|---|---|---|
| 23. | | | |
| 24. | | | |
| 25. | | | |
| 26. | | | |
| 27. | | | |

| Assumption | Consequences if wrong | Certainty | Total of scores in columns 2 and 3 |
|---|---|---|---|
| 28. | | | |
| 29. | | | |
| 30. | | | |
| . . . | | | |

**Debrief (1 hour):** Each team presents its findings for twenty minutes.

**Break (0.25 hour):** While the rest of the team takes a break, the organizer captures the top six critical assumptions.

**Develop a validation plan (2 hours):** Design a validation plan, and determine the seed capital required to test the critical assumptions. What low-cost experiments can you design—and what data should you collect—to test the critical assumptions? How much seed capital do you need to test the assumption? The important principle is, Spend a little and learn a lot. Think of the lowest monetary amount you can request to resolve the critical assumption.

| Top critical assumptions | Validation plan or experiment | Seed capital required |
|---|---|---|
| 1. | | |
| 2. | | |
| 3. | | |

| Top critical assumptions | Validation plan or experiment | Seed capital required |
|---|---|---|
| 4. | | |
| 5. | | |
| 6. | | |

**Debrief (1 hour):** Each team presents its findings for twenty minutes.

**Break (0.25 hour):** While the rest of the participants take a break, the organizer captures the key low-cost experiments and seed capital assumptions.

**Analysis (0.5 hour):** Decide on performance criteria for the dedicated team's critical unknowns.

| Critical unknown | Performance criteria metrics |
|---|---|
| 1. | |
| 2. | |
| 3. | |
| 4. | |

**Wrap-up (0.5 hour):** Note the action items to follow up on. List things that were not completed (e.g., a low-cost experiment for a particular assumption), assign it to the owner, and schedule a follow-up.

**Moving forward:** Every two to four weeks, you'll want to evaluate your leaders and your team using a form like this:

| Performance criteria | Evidence/Notes* |
|---|---|
| Are the critical unknowns clear and well understood? Which are the most uncertain assumptions? The most consequential? | |
| Do changes in plan come out of data that support a clear lesson learned? | |
| Is the innovation leader trying to learn quickly and cheaply? | |
| Is the innovation leader willing to face facts, even when those facts are unpleasant? | |
| Are predictions improving? | |

*Color each row to indicate its state of progress: green for *on track*, yellow for *need to monitor*, and red for *failing*.

# IDEAS IN PRACTICE

When launching NYTD, the team could have used numerous assumptions. Let's look at them grouped by their focus.

## Customer-Centric Assumptions

### Customer

1. The NYTD consumers are those who have internet connections—a narrowband or broadband connection. The company also serves advertisers looking for low-cost alternatives and those with a reputation for trying innovative methods of reaching consumers.

2. Its customer segments are the early adopters, typically aged twenty-one to thirty-five, and *New York Times* followers, typically over thirty-five. The early adopters are interested not only in global news but also in such topics as cars, sports, careers, and managing money. The *New York Times* followers are interested in typical articles they have grown up reading, along with articles on the stock market, home, and gardens.

3. The early adopters are NYTD's important customers to build online market share quickly, as they are the high-growth segment of online users. Narrowband penetration will grow at $X$ percent, and broadband at $Y$ percent.

4. Consumers will not mind being interrupted by advertisements when reading the NYTD version.

## Competitors

5. NYTD's competition is technology companies that have an online presence focused on consumers, such as Microsoft with MSN.com and AOL, as well as other newspapers with plans to have online offerings.

## Value Proposition

6. NYTD will offer users personalized content through market-research competency.

7. The company will bundle the printed newspaper for the *New York Times* followers segment.

## Customer Relationships

8. Users will visit the website several times a day, the product will have multiple touch points with the customer to ensure strong engagement throughout the day.

# Development-Centric Assumptions

## Requirements

9. The online newspaper specification can be implemented as designed in three months.

10. There are ways to track what the users are reading and what features they are using.

11. For the stock market section, there can be a real-time ticker.

### Resources and Capabilities

12. NYTD has the right software—front end and back end—and software engineering resources.

13. Technology architecture, based on Microsoft technologies, will allow scaling to millions of monthly active users and the concurrent handling of tens of thousands of consumers at any given time.

### Activities

14. The NYTD group will build partnerships with a company to host and manage the digital newspaper.

15. NYTD will outsource some tools, such as content management systems.

16. The digital newspaper will work in all existing browsers for all existing versions.

17. To serve different geographical locations, the product will be available in different formats, such as vertical single-page scrolling for China and short, multipage nested format for the United States.

### Partnerships

18. NYTD will partner with internet service providers.

19. It will also partner with content management system providers.

20. NYTD will acquire other special skills by partnering with companies that can generate digital advertisements in various formats, such as banner ads and animated ads.

21. NYTD will obtain real-time stock information from an outside source.

22. NYTD will partner with organizations that can provide a news-group for consumers to discuss opinions and continue the engagement beyond just reading content.

## Monetization-Centric Assumptions

### Cost Structure

23. Labor and equipment (server, connectivity) are the most expensive parts of the business model.

24. An online content management system will cost less than pennies per user.

25. Marketing costs will be $X$ percent of sales for the first year.

### Price

26. NYTD will offer the digital newspaper for free but will charge consumers a certain amount for each premium article. The cost to advertisers will be based on impressions per user and will be discounted by some percentage for the first six months.

### Market

27. The total addressable market (TAM) is $X$ and is based on . . .

28. NYTD will launch the digital product first in the United States, for which the serviceable addressable market is $X$.

29. Share of market by 1999 will be $X$, which is $Y$ percent of the market.

### Fit with Overall Company

30. The internet is a significant, potentially disruptive weak signal that the NYTimes can't afford to miss. Internet adoption is likely to increase at a rate of $X$ percent per year. Of all internet users, $Y$ percent will be NYTD consumers. A large portion of the existing NYTimes consumer base and advertiser base will eventually move to NYTD as consumer behavior and advertising dollars shift online.

## Culling the Critical Assumptions from a Lengthy List

Imagine you are evaluating the thirty assumptions listed above for NYTD. Also assume that you've already tested some of the assumptions in the incubation phase; these are marked with a double dagger (‡) in the following table. Therefore, during the scale phase, you will test the remaining assumptions. In the following table, the assumptions with the highest total score are the most critical—those you should test first. These critical assumptions have been shaded in gray:

| Assumption | Consequences if wrong* | Certainty[†] | Total of scores in columns 2 and 3 |
|---|---|---|---|
| 1. | 5 | 2 | 7‡ |
| 2. | 3 | 3 | 6‡ |
| 3. | 4 | 2 | 6‡ |
| 4. | 4 | 2 | 6 |

| Assumption | Consequences if wrong* | Certainty† | Total of scores in columns 2 and 3 |
|---|---|---|---|
| 5. | 2 | 1 | 3 |
| 6. | 3 | 3 | 6 |
| 7. | 3 | 1 | 4 |
| 8. | 5 | 5 | 10 |
| 9. | 3 | 5 | 8 |
| 10. | 1 | 5 | 6 |
| 11. | 3 | 3 | 6 |
| 12. | 5 | 4 | 9 |
| 13. | 5 | 4 | 9 |
| 14. | 4 | 3 | 7 |
| 15. | 4 | 5 | 9 |
| 16. | 4 | 3 | 7 |
| 17. | 4 | 1 | 5 |
| 18. | 5 | 2 | 7 |
| 19. | 3 | 2 | 5 |
| 20. | 3 | 2 | 5 |
| 21. | 3 | 2 | 5 |
| 22. | 2 | 2 | 4 |
| 23. | 4 | 5 | 9 |
| 24. | 4 | 3 | 7 |
| 25. | 3 | 3 | 6 |
| 26. | 5 | 4 | 9 |

(continued)

| Assumption | Consequences if wrong* | Certainty† | Total of scores in columns 2 and 3 |
|---|---|---|---|
| 27. | 4 | 4 | 8 |
| 28. | 4 | 4 | 8 |
| 29. | 4 | 4 | 8 |
| 30. | 5 | 2 | 7‡ |
| . . . | | | |

* Rate the consequences on a numerical scale of 1 to 5, where 1 is minimal impact and 5 is fatal.
† Rate the certainty of the assumption on a numerical scale of 1 to 5, where 1 is most certain and 5 is least certain.
‡ Assumption has already been assessed in the incubation stage.

## Developing a Validation Plan

Once you have chosen the most critical assumptions, your next step would be to decide on an appropriate low-cost validation plan. The plan involves the design of an experiment that can quickly validate (or invalidate) the assumption with the least amount of seed capital. Here is how you might do this for the NYTD's top six critical assumptions:

| Top critical assumptions | Validation plan or experiment | Seed capital required |
|---|---|---|
| 8. Users will visit the website several times a day, and the product will have multiple touch points with the customer to ensure strong engagement throughout the day. | Schedule customer research visits in consumers' homes. Conduct an experiment similar to IBM's speech-to-text experiment that was detailed in chapter 6, with mock-ups of the real product to test how and when users engage as you shadow them through the day. Do this for both early adopters and *New York Times* followers. | $20K |
| 12. NYTD has the right software—front end and back end—and software engineering resources. | Hire a consultant to (1) benchmark the average costs of building online applications, using comparisons of various companies; (2) identify skills needed for an intact team; (3) list potential intact-team target companies for M&A or partnership. In parallel, analyze internally what it would take to build out such a team organically. Compare the two options. | $10K |

| Top critical assumptions | Validation plan or experiment | Seed capital required |
|---|---|---|
| 13. Technology architecture, based on Microsoft technologies, will allow scaling to millions of monthly active users and the concurrent handling of tens of thousands of consumers at any given time. | Explaining the use case you are building, engage Microsoft and a couple of other vendors to demonstrate, free of charge, the scalability of their products as a prerequisite for adopting the vendor's technologies. For the selected vendor, work on a proof of concept that covers developing custom requirements, if any, for the use case. Jointly target a marketing presentation at a conference for demonstration as a key milestone, forcing function to help get the proof of concept completed, thereby validating this assumption. Furthermore, Microsoft may be interested in preparing and publishing a white paper to promote its technologies. Leverage Microsoft's resources to validate all critical technology unknowns. | $0 |
| 15. NYTD will outsource some tools, such as content management systems. | Talk to the top three providers of online content management, and generate a comparative analysis report for the team. Include product costs, features, and track record of supporting customers. Assess if any provider meets NYTD's requirements of multiple content updates per day, different formats for different geographic areas, and newsgroup integration. | $0 |
| 23. Labor and equipment (server, connectivity) are the most expensive parts of the business model. | Build an end-to-end test system in the lab as a development environment for testing and reproducing bugs. Assess cost structure and how costs will vary as the system becomes a production system and scales with the business. | $50K |
| 26. NYTD will offer the digital newspaper for free but will charge consumers a certain amount for each premium article. The cost to advertisers will be based on impressions per user and will be discounted by some percentage for the first six months. | Send out coupons with the pricing offer, including mock-ups of free and premium content, and ask for a minimum deposit to assess how many people sign up to reveal their preferences (see chapter 6). | $15K |

## Deciding on Performance Criteria

The following table shows the metrics of the performance criteria that could answer a few critical unknowns for the NYTD's Box 3 project:

| Critical unknown | Performance criteria metrics |
| --- | --- |
| Will the market grow? | • Penetration of broadband internet connections<br>• Page views per user per day |
| Can we generate advertising revenues? | • Price per thousand impressions<br>• Ads sold per salesperson per month |
| Can we develop new features of value? | • Page views per new feature<br>• Profitability of new features |

## Using a Performance Scorecard for the Innovation Leader or Team

The following table presents an example of how you or any other leader might assess the performance of your Box 3 scaling efforts. Note that each row has been shaded to indicate the state of progress: white [green] for *on track*, light gray [yellow] for *need to monitor*, and dark gray [red] for *failing*. In practice, it is better to use the colors suggested in the brackets to make the status more visible:

| Performance criteria | Metrics | Evidence/notes |
| --- | --- | --- |
| Are the critical unknowns clear and well understood? Which are the most uncertain assumptions and the most consequential? | Reviewed by team and sent to everybody in weekly status emails | Team reviewed critical unknowns in planning meetings every three weeks for the last two months, and meeting notes were documented and sent out. |

| Performance criteria | Metrics | Evidence/notes |
|---|---|---|
| Do changes in the plan come out of data that supports a clear lesson learned? | Approval meetings, with decisions and changes documented on SharePoint site for the team | Approval meetings were canceled last month because of the leadership team's lack of availability. Remedy: Add a delegate when the innovation leader is absent, with the authority to make decisions. |
| Is the innovation leader trying to learn quickly and cheaply? | Number of experiments under budget relative to learning | Funding goals are on track for three experiments, but expenses for hiring external consultants seem to be coming in higher than expected. |
| Is the innovation leader willing to face facts, even when those facts are unpleasant? | Leader communicating, up the chain to management, the bad news as fast as the good | In face-to-face meetings with the Box 1 leader, the innovation leader presented a slide on lessons learned, failures, risks, and progress. |
| Are predictions improving? | Plotted trends showing marked improvement in predictions | Costs trending flat; some predictions are getting better, but others need diagnosis. Remedy: Discuss at the next learning review. |

*Note:* Each row has been shaded to indicate its status: white for *on track*, light gray for *need to monitor*, and dark gray for *failing*.

# Wrap-Up

Since it is based on weak signals, Box 3 is nothing more than a series of assumptions. For this reason, every innovation carries a series of risks. This chapter covered several ways to address these risks most effectively.

- The learn challenge is about testing critical assumptions. Spend to reduce risk.

- Testing does cost money, but with a methodical, thoughtful approach outlined in this chapter, you can test your assumptions without spending excessive resources.

- The golden rule is, Spend a little, learn a lot.

# 10

# WRAP-UP

Executing Box 3 innovation in any established organization is a Herculean task. Yet it is a necessary task for transforming your organization to earn and maintain its leadership in the future. Box 3 execution requires a different organizational logic and a different execution methodology. Every Box 3 experiment faces a forget challenge, a borrow challenge, and a learn challenge. You must overcome these three challenges to eventually see disproportionate profits relative to your investments. While Box 3 profits are the ultimate measure of success, two other metrics can help you assess whether this playbook is having a meaningful impact.

First is the mind-set shift. Without education or training, Box 1 and Box 3 teams fall into the trap of personalizing the conflicts that naturally emerge, given the different jobs the organization is trying to do. Creating the conditions for change, where the two leaders and their teams can manage the conflicts for the betterment of the entire company, is winning 50 percent or more of the innovation execution battle.

The second metric is the incorporation of the tools presented in this playbook in your company's systems, planning, and culture. If you do this, your organization will develop new competencies and muscles to accelerate Box 3 innovation efforts that will invariably either acquire momentum or fall by the wayside, overpowered by the tyranny of the urgent. Integrating the methods learned in this playbook is the remaining piece in winning the innovation execution battle.

Given the exponential rate of change in the external environment, companies have no alternative but to adapt. Shifting the organization's mind-set and complementing it with the tools presented in this book will ultimately help change your organization's behavior. We strongly recommend that you do not "boil the ocean" by starting to incorporate processes through directives without piloting a Box 3 first. It is best to pilot these projects in one to three initiatives, share the learning, tweak the processes for your organization's circumstances, and then embed them into your DNA. To succeed, you must not only scope the pilot initiative to something tangible and manageable, but also obtain the sponsorship of senior Box 1 and Box 3 leaders for the pilots. Finally, you ought to drive the project's adoption by taking steps to reduce people's resistance to it. At the same time, you'll inspire teams through credibility built on interim successes along the journey.

As a final exercise, we ask you to reflect on three questions:

What key takeaways did you and your leadership team gain from using this playbook?

_____

_____

_____

_____

_____

_____

_____

_____

_____

_____

_____

_____

What actions will you and your leadership team take?

_____

_____

_____

_____

_____

_____

_____

_____

_____

_____

What are you and your leadership team going to teach others in your organization?

_____

_____

_____

_____

_____

_____

_____

_____

_____

_____

_____

_____

_____

After you answer these questions, fill in the following table to predict the three next actions your team will take and their expected results over the next thirty days:

| Next actions | Expected results |
|---|---|
| 1. | |

| Next actions | Expected results |
|---|---|
| 2. | |
| 3. | |

**Next learning review for me and my team scheduled for (date)** _____

Then, as you continue the three-box journey, compare your expected results with your predictions *every* month. If your predictions are improving, then you'll know you are learning!

# Appendix

## SAMPLE QUESTIONS ABOUT CRITICAL ASSUMPTIONS FOR MEETING ATTENDEES

When planning to scale your Box 3 project, you need to assemble your team to identify the critical customer-centric, development-centric, and monetization-centric assumptions or unknowns that the team will test in the near future. A day or more before the meeting, distribute this handout with the following questions about critical assumptions so the attendees can become familiar with them prior to the meeting.[1] You can tailor these questions to your company's business or add your own. The meeting attendees don't need to answer any of the questions yet. Inform them that they will work together at the meeting, in preassigned teams, to answer the questions.

## Overview

The strategic intent of our [Box 3 initiative name] is to get to a [$B] business by [date]. To realize this intent, what critical unknowns/assumptions must we test in the next twelve months?[2] Consider these generic types of unknowns in the following categories:

1. **Customer-centric**: Does the customer want it?

2. **Development-centric:** Can we build it?

3. **Monetization-centric:** Can we make money?

4. **Strategic fit:** Is this strategic to the company?

## 1. Customer-Centric Assumptions

### Customer

- Who is our customer?

- What are our customer segments (e.g., those that require different value from the offering, are reached through different distribution channels, require different types of relationships, have substantially different profitability)?

- Who are our most important customers?

- Do we correctly understand the customer problem for every customer segment?

- Which of our customers' needs are we satisfying or which customer problems are we solving?

## Competitors

- Who is our competition today (e.g., companies that provide similar value or alternative options that customers use today to get a job done [that we are trying to displace])?

- Who will enter the market? How will competition affect demand for our products?

## Value Proposition

- What value do we provide to the customer unlike/better than our competitors (e.g., new features, price, brand, performance, scale, customization, risk reduction, cost reduction, design, time to market)?

- What bundle of products and services are we offering to each customer segment?

## Channels

- Through which channels do our customers want to be reached? How are we reaching them now?

- How are our channels integrated?

- Which channels are the most cost-efficient?

- How are we integrating our channels with customer workflows?

- Is a direct or indirect distribution strategy best?

## Customer Relationships

- What type of relationship does each of our customer segments want to maintain with us (e.g., joint creation and tight integration, dedicated personal assistance, as a dual-source commodity supplier)?

- Do we have relationships at the right decision-making levels to provide relevant feedback or are we talking to customers' R&D teams when the buying decision is elsewhere in the organization?

## 2. Development-Centric Assumptions

### Requirements

- Do we understand the customer specification? Is it well defined?

### Resources and Capabilities

- Do we have the right key resources (financial, IP, human, physical assets/systems, technology) to deliver?

- What are the technology or architecture unknowns?

### Activities

- What key activities do our value propositions require?

- Do we have the right value chain architecture?

- Do we have the means for production and problem solving?

- What key activities are required for our platform dependencies?

- What key activities are required for our distribution channels, customer relationships, and revenue streams?

### Partnerships

- Who are our key partners? What resources are we getting from them? What key activities do they perform?

- Who are our key suppliers? What do we get from them?

## 3. Monetization-Centric Assumptions

### Cost Structure

- Which costs in our business model are the most expensive?

- Which key resources are the most expensive?

- Which key activities are the most expensive?

- What are our fixed costs? Our variable costs?

- What are our overhead costs?

- What cost advantage can we get with economies of scale and economies of scope?

- How does our cost structure compare with that of competitors?

### Price

- What is our target price? What is our customer's willingness to pay?

- How does our pricing compare with that of competitors?

### Market

- What is our total addressable market (TAM)?

- What is our serviceable addressable market (SAM)?

- What is our share of market (SOM)?

- How long is our sustainable advantage?

- How long is the market window to capitalize on the opportunity?

## 4. Fit with the Overall Company

- Is this project strategic to the company?

# NOTES

## Chapter 1

1. Blockbuster Inc., *Form 10-K for Fiscal Year Ended December 31, 2004* (Washington, DC: United States Securities and Exchange Commission, 2005).

2. Nvidia Corporation, "Nvidia Announces Financial Results for Second Quarter Fiscal 2019," August 16, 2018, https://nvidianews.nvidia.com/news /nvidia-announces-financial-results-for-second-quarter-fiscal-2019.

3. Nathaniel Meyersohn, "Walmart Thinks Shopping via Text Might Be Retail's Next Big Thing," *CNN Business*, November 8, 2018, www.cnn.com/2018/11/08/business /walmart-jetblack-shopping-retail/index.html.

4. Liz Carey, "One-Fifth of U.S. Newspapers Close in Last 14 years," *Daily Yonder*, October 22, 2018, www.dailyyonder.com/one-fifth-u-s-newspapers-close-last-14-years /2018/10/22/28144.

5. The March 1995 market cap is unavailable. We approximated it based on the New York Times Company's March 31, 1995, 10-Q filing.

## Chapter 2

1. Kiddle, "How Is Kiddle Designed Specifically for Kids?," www.kiddle.co/about.php.

2. Alan Levin and Bloomberg, "Amazon Reveals Its Latest Delivery Drone Design," *Fortune*, June 5, 2019.

## Chapter 3

1. Gary Hamel and C. K. Prahalad, "Strategic Intent," *Harvard Business Review*, July–August 2005, https://hbr.org/2005/07/strategic-intent.

2. John F. Kennedy, "Address to Joint Session of Congress, May 25, 1961," TNC:200, John F. Kennedy Presidential Library and Museum, www.jfklibrary.org/learn/about-jfk /historic-speeches/address-to-joint-session-of-congress-may-25-1961.

3. Personal communication with the author.

4. "Our Path Forward," New York Times Company, October 7, 2015, https://nytco -assets.nytimes.com/m/Our-Path-Forward.pdf.

5. Amanda Walgrove, "The Explosive Growth of Online Video, in 5 Charts," *Contently*, July 6, 2015, https://contently.com/2015/07/06/the-explosive-growth-of -online-video-in-5-charts.

6. Eric Bellman, "Indians Are So Crazy about Mobile Video, They Use YouTube Like Google," *Wall Street Journal*, January 21, 2019, www.wsj.com/articles/indians-are-binge -watching-mobile-videos-pushing-youtube-others-to-innovate-11548079230?mod =searchresults&page=1&pos=2.

## Chapter 5

1. We wrote about this in Vijay Govindarajan and Manish Tangri, "Toddler Engineering," *Times of India* (Crest edition), February 23, 2013.

2. George Land and Beth Jarman, *Breakpoint and Beyond: Mastering the Future Today* (New York: HarperBusiness, 1992).

3. Ibid.

4. Isha Tangri is the daughter of Manish, who asked her this question in February 2019, when she was nine years old. We thank her for her cooperation.

## Chapter 6

1. These three categories are adapted from IDEO's trifecta of desirability, feasibility, and viability categories for eliminating market risk, technology risk, and business risk. For more information, go to IDEO, "Design Thinking Defined," https://designthinking .ideo.com.

2. Michael J. Gelb and Sarah Miller Caldicott, *Innovate Like Edison* (New York: Penguin Group, 2007).

3. Jeffrey Van Camp, "Review: Jibo Social Robot," *Wired*, November 7, 2017, www.wired.com/2017/11/review-jibo-social-robot.

4. Jesus Diaz, "One of the Decade's Most Hyped Robots Sends Its Farewell Message," *Fast Company*, March 6, 2019; "Jibo Makes *Time*'s Best Inventions of 2017," November 21, 2017, www.jibo.com/jibo-makes-times-best-inventions-2017.

5. Andrew Clarke, "Lessons from Webvan," Ground Floor Partners, https:// groundfloorpartners.com/lessons-from-webvan.

6. Julie L. Davis and Suzanne S. Harrison, *Edison in the Boardroom: How Leading Companies Realize Value from Their Intellectual Assets* (Hoboken, NJ: Wiley, 2001).

7. Venture capitalist Ben Horowitz's 2015 commencement address at Columbia University's Fu Foundation School of Engineering and Applied Science mentioned that Airbnb's founder, Brian Chesky, studied and relied on the historical fact that in the past, people stayed at other people's houses as part of the concept for his company. "It's What You Can Contribute," address by Ben Horowitz, YouTube video, posted June 1, 2015, https://www.youtube.com/watch?v=WRYRBGX4lVM

8. Drake Baer, "The Making of Tesla: Invention, Betrayal, and the Birth of the Roadster," *Business Insider*, November 11, 2014, www.businessinsider.com/tesla-the -origin-story-2014-10.

9. This example is adapted from Jeremy Clark, *Pretotyping@Work: Invent like a Startup, Invest like a Grownup* (Seattle: Amazon Digital Services, 2012; Kindle edition).

10. Elon Musk, "Foundation 20: Elon Musk," interview with Kevin Rose, YouTube video, posted September 7, 2012, www.youtube.com/watch?v=L-s_3b5fRd8.

11. Corning Incorporated, "A Day Made of Glass . . . Made Possible by Corning," YouTube video, posted February 7, 2011, www.youtube.com/watch?v=6Cf7IL_eZ38.

## Chapter 7

1. Vijay Govindarajan and Chris Trimble, *The Other Side of Innovation: Solving the Execution Challenge* (Boston: Harvard Business Review Press, 2011), discussed in "Executing Innovation," *Business Standard*, January 21, 2013, www.business-standard .com/article/management/executing-innovation-110091300001_1.html.

2. Alex Davies, "GM's Cruise Rolls Back Its Target for Self-Driving Cars," *Wired*, July 24, 2019, https://www.wired.com/story/gms-cruise-rolls-back-target-self-driving-cars/.

## Appendix

1. Adapted from Wikipedia, "Business Model Canvas," https://en.wikipedia.org/wiki/ Business_Model_Canvas.

2. A good source for a generic list of assumptions is Scott Anthony, Mark Johnson, et al., *The Innovator's Guide to Growth* (Boston, MA: Harvard Business Review Press, 2008).

# INDEX

# ACKNOWLEDGMENTS

### From VG Govindarajan

In my previous books I have gone to great lengths to acknowledge every contributor. This book is no different in that the number of individuals involved is large. Nevertheless, I'd like to make an exception in this case so that I may focus on three distinct events that brought about significant changes in my career.

First was my admission to Harvard Business School to pursue an MBA. The mission of Harvard Business School is to "educate leaders who make a difference in the world." HBS shaped my passion to impact the broader world.

Second was being granted tenure at Dartmouth's Tuck School of Business. Tuck provided me with the resources to pursue scholarly research that has had an impact on the practice of management.

Third has been my association with over forty CEOs of *Fortune* 500 companies. Most recently, I worked with PepsiCo's former CEO and Chairperson, Indra K. Nooyi. Every one of the CEOs I've known has made me a better professor—and a better person.

### From Manish Tangri

The idea for this book originated with VG, my coauthor, my professor, my mentor, my friend. VG, thank you from the bottom of my heart for giving me the opportunity to work on this book, for recognizing the value of my corporate experience in broadening the three-box framework's impact, and for motivating me to share my knowledge with the world.

To my parents and parents-in-law, thank you for your blessings.

To my wife Arti, thank you for covering for me on all those evenings and weekends when the book took me away. Your unconditional support is what made this book possible. To my daughter Isha, thanks not only for your contribution to the book but also for sharing my excitement every step of the way. To my daughter Siyona, thanks not only for your contagious joviality but also for your willingness to sacrifice our playtime in order to help me meet my schedule. Thank you, Puneet, Shivani, Akash, Viraj, Ankit, Bhavana, Shanaya, Eva, and Babli. I am very fortunate to have each of you in my life, and I am eternally grateful for your love, for your respect, and for your always being there for me.

Sincere thanks to the late Sarah Caldicott, the great-grandniece of Thomas Edison, for helping me understand Edison's mind-set toward innovation.

This book is the culmination of my multidecade journey in exploring growth and innovation. Needless to say, I am immensely thankful to my hundreds of fellow travelers from Microsoft, Eaton, and Intel as well as the Tuck community and my thousand-plus LinkedIn connections who walked a few steps with me along the way. The projects we did together, the knowledge we shared, as well as the partnerships and mentorships, all helped build my judgment and business acumen.

### From VG and Manish

We could not have found a better adviser, ally, and friend than our editor at Harvard Business Review Press, Kevin Evers.

Most important, we want to thank you, our readers, for your interest in this book. Our hope is that you can use the insights from both books—*The Three-Box Solution* and *The Three-Box Solution Playbook*—to lead innovation for the future while you maintain excellence in the present. We hope you share our enthusiasm for building Box 3 businesses within established organizations, and we welcome your comments. You can reach Vijay Govindarajan at vg@dartmouth.edu and Manish Tangri at operationalizinginnovation@gmail.com

# ABOUT THE AUTHORS

**Vijay Govindarajan (VG)** is widely regarded as one of the world's leading experts on strategy and innovation. VG is the Coxe Distinguished Professor (a Dartmouth-wide faculty chair) at the Tuck School of Business at Dartmouth College and a former Marvin Bower Fellow at Harvard Business School. He is a Faculty Partner in Mach 49, a Silicon Valley incubator. He was the first Professor in Residence and Chief Innovation Consultant at General Electric. He worked with General Electric CEO Jeff Immelt to write "How GE Is Disrupting Itself," the *Harvard Business Review* article that pioneered the concept of reverse innovation: any innovation that is adopted first in the developing world. HBR picked reverse innovation as one of the "Great Moments in Management" in the last century. VG is a *New York Times* and *Wall Street Journal* best-selling author and a two-time winner of the prestigious McKinsey Award for the best article published in *Harvard Business Review*. He was named by Thinkers 50 as a Top 3 Management Thinker in the world, received the Breakthrough Innovation Award in 2011, and was inducted into the Thinkers 50 Hall of Fame in 2019.

VG has been identified as a leading management thinker by influential publications, including Outstanding Faculty, named by *Business Week* in its *Guide to the Best Business Schools*; Top Ten Business School Professor in Corporate Executive Education, named by *Business Week*; Top Five Most Respected Executive Coaches on Strategy, rated by *Forbes*; Rising Super Star, cited by the *Economist*; Outstanding Teacher of the Year, voted by MBA students.

Before joining the faculty at Tuck, VG was on the faculties of Harvard Business School, INSEAD (Fontainebleau), and the Indian Institute of Management (Ahmedabad, India).

The recipient of numerous awards for excellence in research, VG was inducted into the *Academy of Management Journal*'s Hall of Fame and ranked by *Management International Review* as one of the Top 20 North American Superstars for research in strategy. One of his papers was recognized as one of the ten most-cited articles in the entire fifty-year history of the *Academy of Management Journal*.

VG is a rare faculty member who has published more than twenty articles in top academic journals (*Academy of Management Journal, Academy of Management Review, Strategic Management Journal*) and more than twenty articles in prestigious practitioner journals, including several best-selling *Harvard Business Review* articles. He published *Reverse Innovation,* a *New York Times* and *Wall Street Journal* best seller.

VG has worked with CEOs and top management teams in more than 30 percent of the *Fortune* 500 firms to discuss, challenge, and escalate their thinking about strategy. His clients include Boeing, Coca-Cola, Colgate, Deere, FedEx, GE, Hewlett-Packard, IBM, J.P. Morgan Chase, Johnson & Johnson, New York Times, Procter & Gamble, Sony, and Walmart. He has been a keynote speaker in the *Business Week* CEO Forum, HSM World Business Forum, TED, and World Economic Forum at Davos.

VG received his doctorate from Harvard Business School and was awarded the Robert Bowne Prize for the best thesis proposal. He received his MBA with distinction from the Harvard Business School. VG received his Chartered Accountancy degree in India, where he was awarded the President's Gold Medal for obtaining the first rank nationwide.

**Manish Tangri** has been driving strategy and growth initiatives at Intel Corporation for over a decade. At Intel Capital, he leads M&A strategy and execution of strategic transactions—mergers and acquisitions, equity investments, and partnerships—worldwide. His expertise spans such areas as software, security, computer vision, artificial intelligence, self-driving cars, and data-center technologies, including field-programmable gate arrays and silicon photonics. In his previous role, he was Director of Strategic Business Development at Intel's Perceptual Computing Group, part of the New Technology Division. One of the early employees (number six) on the Intel Perceptual Computing team, he spent five years doing deals to obtain new capabilities from outside Intel as the team grew to more than seven hundred people at one time. His strategic business development activities exposed him to several verticals: technology (software, services, biometrics, biosensing); security and authentication; health; edutainment; robotics and drones; and hundreds of companies therein. He gained insights into emerging trends by meeting with domain experts at top universities and research centers in the United States and Europe, such as the Massachusetts Institute of Technology Media Lab, Dartmouth College, University of California at Berkeley, Stanford University, the MIT Lincoln Laboratory, Imperial College, ETH Zurich, Technical University of Munich, and National Aeronautics and Space Administration. Previously, he rotated across Intel in various entrepreneurial, functional, and operational roles, such as ecosystem marketing, brand strategy, and new-business strategic planning.

Passionate about innovation, Manish has led division-wide innovation activities in Intel's PC Client Group, the company's largest division at the time. He has worked with industry innovation experts such as Sarah Caldicott, great-grandniece of Thomas Edison, and Vijay Govindarajan, Manish's coauthor and the author of the *New York Times* best seller *Reverse Innovation*. Manish's publications include *Harvard Business Review* blogs and an out-of-the-box section newspaper article in India's premier newspaper *Times of India* (Crest Edition). In the late 2010s, he also led activities to educate Intel's top executives on methods for accelerating innovation execution and applying the methods across various key initiatives at the company.

Manish is also passionate about teaching. Since 2014, as an adjunct faculty member at Santa Clara University's Leavey School of Business, Manish has cultivated MBA students by teaching them innovation and strategic business development concepts. He currently teaches a four-unit, self-developed course called Accelerating Innovation that also includes three-box concepts. For more than five years, he taught Intel University's Strengthening Manager Skills course to company managers and was twice recognized as top instructor out of nine thousand. He was not only a regular guest speaker at the Tuck School of Business's entrepreneurship class but also ran training workshops for Intel's PC division's top hundred leaders and top thirty creative individuals.

Previously, Manish spent almost a decade at Microsoft Corporation in four product units in a variety of business contexts—two startups, one turnaround, and one realignment—and received three patent awards. He led the engineering team responsible for www.msn.com across twenty-one global markets. His other experience includes serving as an assistant to CEO role and stints at Eaton Corporation, Chase Doors, Hughes Network Systems, and Analytical Services and Materials. He has an MS in Computer Science and Engineering from Michigan State University and an MBA from the Tuck School of Business at Dartmouth.